THE GREY LADY

AND OTHER STORIES AND STUFF

BY THE SAME AUTHOR

Making a Comprehensive Work:
the Road from Bomb Alley (Blackwell 1981)

Teachers and Teaching (Blackwell 1984)

Why Preach? (Foundery Press 2000)

A Short History of the Employment Appeal Tribunal
(Moorley's Publishing 2002, reprinted 2004)

Short stories published by Scotforth Books
on behalf of the author:

Messages (2011)
Never Was There Tale of Brighter Hue (2013)

THE GREY LADY

AND OTHER STORIES AND STUFF

Peter Dawson

Ken,
Love to you & Betty.
Age takes its toll but
we are still having a
great time.

Grace & Peace,
Peter

First published in 2015 on behalf of the author by
Scotforth Books, Carnegie House,
Chatsworth Road, Lancaster LA1 4SL

ISBN 13: 978-1-909817-21-0

Printed in the UK by Printondemand–worldwide.com

About the Author

Peter Dawson, a graduate of the LSE, was for ten years the headmaster of an Inner London mixed comprehensive school for two thousand pupils. His account of that was a best-seller in 1981: *Making a Comprehensive Work: the Road from Bomb Alley.* He was subsequently the General Secretary of the Professional Association of Teachers, the leader of a team of Ofsted school inspectors and a UK delegate to the economic and social assembly of the EC in Brussels. He was appointed an OBE for services to education in 1986, then served for twelve years as a lay member of the Employment Appeal Tribunal in London, hearing appeals against the findings of local employment tribunals. A regular newspaper columnist and broadcaster in his heyday, he is an ordained Minister of the Methodist Church with evangelical tendencies. Happily and securely married for over fifty years, he is a sponsor of the Family Education Trust, which promotes traditional family values.

CONTENTS

	Page
Introduction	ix
The Grey Lady	1
On Writing	7
Molly's Shed	9
Politics	15
Charlotte Makes a Move	17
How the Young See Others	23
Sticky Wicket	25
Teenagers	33
Napoleon Smith and the Vulture	35
Be Careful What You Say	43
We Need to Talk	45
John Donne	49
My Father Judah	51
Holocaust Haiku	57
Unforgettable	59
Leaving Auschwitz	65

Big Day at the Palace	67
Religion	75
As You Like It	77
Rules for Teachers	81
Spongiform Schooling	83
School to University	87
Paul Robeson Plays Othello	89
History	93
Serving Europe	95
Advice from the Famous	99
Generation Born to Lose	101
Courtship and After	105
On Being Disabled	107
The Church	111
Word Games	113
Getting On	121
Human Sexuality	123
Leadership	127
The Classroom is a Stage	129
Coming to a Conclusion	131
Issues in Education	133
Somebody's Child	145

INTRODUCTION

In this third collection of my stories, some are fictional and some auto-biographical. It will be clear to readers from its contents to which category a story belongs. My having earned a living in education and education politics, a good deal of the material has to do with that.

There is further stuff in this collection. After each story, there is a page or two of quotations accumulated over a lifetime of reading, teaching, going to see great plays, addressing meetings on education and associated subjects, leading public worship and arguing the toss with whoever was up for an exchange of opinions.

In this further feature, you will find a rich tapestry of utterances. My personal favourite is Jill Tweedie's brilliantly perceptive verdict on journalism as an activity in which today's mo joost (sic) is tomorrow's drawer lining. Second favourite is the boxer Muhammad Ali's assertion, while being interviewed by Harry Carpenter on television: 'I don't always know what I'm talking about, but I know I'm right.' Perhaps most moving is Primo

Levi's account, entitled *Leaving Auschwitz*, of an old lady's survival after challenging Adolf Hitler.

There has stood on my desk for more than fifty years some words of a writer who lived five hundred years before Christ trod planet Earth. His name was Aeschylus and he wrote: 'Men are not made for safe havens.' Perhaps some traces of that conviction will be found in the pages that follow.

Peter Dawson
Spring 2015

THE GREY LADY

They blamed Sister Brimmington for the story in the papers. Mr Gordon, one of the consultants, said she had always been too garrulous.

The year was 1973 and young Nurse Aitken was a rather naive newcomer to St Peter's Hospital, in her first appointment since qualifying. She didn't understand what the consultant meant so quietly inquired of a rather good-looking medical student who came to the ward from time to time what being garrulous was all about. 'He means Sister talks too much', he said, 'Garrulous is from the Latin word for chatter. Didn't you do Latin at school?'

The girl smiled. 'Milford Comprehensive wasn't that sort of school, You were lucky if you got a good teacher for anything. Some of them couldn't keep order in a cemetery. If I hadn't left to go to sixth form college, I would never have got into nursing and ended up here', she said.

'Well, I'm glad you did', said Tony Evans, smiling down upon the girl. She blushed, her white cap emphasizing the scarlet hue of her face. 'But it's a bit scary, this story in the papers, isn't it?' she said. 'Look', said the young man, inwardly resolving to get to know this slight, elfin creature better, 'every hospital has a grey lady. Some say she saves lives. She is benign.'

'Benign?' said the girl. 'From the Latin benigna, meaning kindly, gentle,' came the reply. Jenny Aitken thought to herself that she must seem a fool to this nice young chap. Sad.

Later, Tony asked his friend and fellow medic, James Holland, if he had noticed Nurse Aitken on the children's ward. 'Hullo, hullo!', said James, laughing, 'Are you allowing your interest to stray from your medical studies? Didn't you know that sixty-three point five per cent of medical students fail to qualify because of getting involved with girls?' 'Absolute rubbish!' declared his friend, 'Where did you get that figure from?' 'I made it up', replied James, still laughing.

The story in the papers had begun when the parents of little Bonnie Jenkins, just one year old, had written to the local paper to applaud the standard of care their baby daughter had received at St Peter's. The editor had assigned an experienced reporter, Bob Riches, to chase the story. He rang the chief executive of the hospital for leave to bring a press photographer in. 'We want to write a big hooray story about St Peter's. Don't tell me you wouldn't like that!', he declared.

Robert Staples, the chief executive, thought to himself it was time there was some good news coming out of the health service. He laid down some ground rules. 'You wouldn't be able to take pictures on the ward', he told the reporter, 'but you could interview Sister Brimmington, who's in charge there. If you want a shot of a baby, you could get one of Bonnie Jenkins at home. I'm sure her parents will agree.' And so the stage was set for a drama destined to make St Peter's Hospital the talk of Bindleford, a country town, and beyond.

On the first Monday in April 1973, a double spread in the centre pages of the *Bindleford News* carried a picture of Bonnie Jenkins and her delighted parents, and one of Sister Doris Brimmington – Sister B, as she was often known in the hospital, where she had served for nearly thirty years. A woman of motherly disposition, she cared deeply for her nurses. But her kindliness evaporated if one of them was not up to the job. Honest and open of manner, and never having been interviewed by the media before, she let it be known that baby Bonnie was lucky to be alive.

'One of my nurses didn't understand decimals', she said, smiling. 'When that baby girl should have been given half a mil of medicine, she was almost given five mil. The nurse thought point five meant five. But it was all right. The Grey Lady put her hand on the nurse's arm and stopped her. The nurse was terrified and came running to me. I went and dealt with it, then explained to the nurse about the Grey Lady. She has saved a few lives over the years,' she said, 'I'm so glad she is around at St Peter's.'

Bindleford was agog when the story appeared with Sister B's very words beside her picture. Bob Riches knew the paper had a story likely to get national coverage, and his editor agreed. By the day following publication, three national papers had sent experienced reporters to the hospital. BBC cameras arrived in the hospital forecourt.

Offshoots of the story ran for ten days before the media decided they had exhausted it. There had been television programmes on the training of nurses, on the teaching of mathematics in schools and on paranormal activity of all kinds.

One of the Sunday newspapers devoted its coloured magazine to stories from no fewer than fourteen hospitals of activity by a grey lady. The most prestigious was St Thomas' Hospital in London, on the south bank of the Thames, looking out over the river at the Houses of Parliament. Here Florence Nightingale first established a school of nursing. Unsurprisingly, belief in the spectral presence of Florence, overseeing nurses in training, was shared by many.

The team that carried out the research won a press award. What they discovered was a widespread belief in the hospital service that a ghostly grey lady would appear if a nurse was about to threaten a patient's life by the maladmistration of medication. Some said she was an apparition of Florence Nightingale. The commonest belief was that a grey lady was a dominant nursing figure from a hospital's past. When Sister Brimmington read this, she warned her nurses that she would come back and haunt them if they didn't watch out.

Tony Evans' friend James Holland, whose sketching of body parts was much admired by his fellow medics, was something of a prankster. He created a black and white line drawing of a nurse in an old-fashioned long dress and apron, a nurse's cap and a cloak. He had the figure emerging rather spookily from a mist. He hung it in the entrance lobby of the nurses' residential accommodation.

'Well', said Tony Evans to Jenny Aitken as they bumped into one another in the hospital restaurant, 'the Grey Lady certainly got us some news coverage. St Peter's has had its moment of fame.' The girl smiled knowingly and said, 'It's all to the good. The Grey Lady is benign.' She paused then added, 'That word comes from the Latin, you know. Benigna. Kind and gentle.' Tony laughed. He thought to himself that this girl was adorable.

A voice with a strong Welsh lilt sounded. 'Ooer. Hark at our Jenny. Showing off, isn't it?' It was Eleri Jones, one of Jenny's nursing colleagues on the children's ward. She had more to say. 'We didn't do Latin at Merthyr Secondary Modern. We were saved from that. Weren't too keen on English either', she said, screaming with laughter. 'Sorry, Jenny,' she added. 'Don't mean to put you down when you're with your boy friend.' She looked Tony up and down. 'He's proper handsome, isn't it? Like Cary Grant.' She laughed again as she moved away.

Jenny was blushing just as she had done when she had first spoken to Tony. 'Sorry about her. She's a Welsh windbag', she explained. 'Don't be sorry', said the young medical student, 'I like the idea of being your boy friend. How about it?' And so it came about that Tony Evans and Jenny Aitken became, as they say, an item.

Eight years later, married with children, a drawing of a nurse half hidden in a grey mist hung in their home. It was entitled: *The Grey Lady*. The drawing was a gift from James Holland, Tony's best man at his wedding to Jenny. Asked about the misty figure by visitors, Tony would say, 'She sort of brought us together and watches over us.' Jenny would add, smiling, 'Her influence is benign.'

On Writing

A good book is a precious life's blood.

Thomas Carlyle

*In journalism, today's mo joost (sic) is
tomorrow's drawer lining.*

Jill Tweedie

*Could you not, to encourage us also-rans,
print an occasional obituary on one or two
failures? A monthly 'nothing much to report'
obituary would do wonders for us.*

Richard Langley to the Daily Telegraph

*In Italy during the Second World War, I
had been wounded and my father, a stickler
for correct English, received a telegram
saying I had been hospitalized. He wrote me
saying, 'My God! They've changed you into a
hospital.'*

Spike Milligan to the Sunday Times

The extraordinary question that the sixteenth century French writer Montaigne provokes in the reader over and over again is, 'How does he know so much about me?'

Bernard Levin

If Benjamin Spock had not written his permissive book on parenting entitled 'Baby and Child Care', there would have been no need for him to publish the sequel, 'Bringing Up Children in a Difficult Time'.

Anon

Written by an eleven-year-old in the back of a worn copy of 'South with Scott' by Edward Evans, an account of Scott's attempt to reach the South Pole in 1911/12:

This book, I think, is only suitable for children about 13 or 14. It is hard to read and very boring.

MOLLY'S SHED

Everyone called it the shed, although the sign over the front of the café said Molly's. It was darkly tucked under the railway bridge at the bottom of Villiers Street at Charing Cross. At night, it became part of cardboard city, where the flotsam and jetsam of society slept in cardboard boxes. For just a few coppers, or for nothing if she felt that someone was truly destitute, Molly would offer a mug of strong tea and a thick slice of bread spread with margarine to anyone who negotiated a way between the boxes on the pavement, from which snores emanated, to the door of her place. She did a good deal of her business at night.

Molly reckoned Ralph McTell was thinking of the shed when he wrote his song about the streets of London. She had old women who came in carrying everything they had in two carrier bags. She also had old men who spent ages looking at the world over the rim of a mug of tea and dreaming of better days.

Molly, a big woman with a voice like the north wind in winter, had had a difficult life. She had been married at a young age to a loser who left her destitute after a couple of years. She was young and shapely in those days and went on the game in Soho for several years, then got a job selling cheap souvenirs to tourists from a stall by Trafalgar Square. She worked as a cleaner at the Strand Palace Hotel for several years after that. Her luck turned when she won some money on the lottery, which she used to buy the cafe. It was a ramshackle place which cost her next to nothing but she did it up herself. 'It's my little haven', she would say, 'I'm cosy here in my little shed, just like Ken. I will survive'.

The only person with whom Molly had ever been close was her brother Ken. He had been a quiet, undemonstrative little man. His domineering wife and raucous children got him down. A highly skilled worker in wood, he built himself a large garden shed as a workshop and spent most of his time there making beautiful pieces of furniture with which he filled the family home. When the children grew up and left and his wife died, Ken moved his bed into the shed and spent even more time there. Breathing in the aroma of wood shavings as he lay down to sleep was a delight he had longed for. One morning he did not wake up. The expression on his face was blissful.

Molly ran her battered old café along very strict lines. Although her customers might have been regarded as riff raff by society, she would not admit drunks or thieves. She knew the petty criminal fraternity around Charing Cross well and would show the door to any who turned up. She was on good terms with the local fuzz who would sometimes direct shop-door sleepers in the Strand to Molly's. 'Go down Villiers Street and ask for the shed', they would say. Many an old man or woman of no interest to the passing world had sat in Molly's shed with a cup of hot soup and stayed alive against their expectations in bitter winter weather.

Some local politicians did not approve of Molly. 'She attracts layabouts and unwashed hasbeens', said Councillor Jenkins, a man of rigorously aesthetic principles. 'Not so much hasbeens as neverwases', chuckled Councillor Ranji, who owned seven restaurants specializing in high class Indian cuisine. 'Can't we clear the old girl out and get rid of that pack of nobodies she harbours?' he asked.

But there were other voices with a different messages. 'So where would the rough sleepers go?', said one. 'Actually, Molly is a sort of social worker. She looks after down and outs', said another. 'We don't want them dying on the streets', responded a third. Councillor Rattenbury, an ordained minister of the Baptist Church, who often visited Molly's place when in the area, said: 'We ought to be funding the shed, and places like it.' There was an eruption of fury from the close-her-down brigade.

At the end of a heated discussion, a customary political decision was made, namely to do nothing and wait and see what happened.

What happened was that the shed was burnt down one night. Molly's safe haven, which was also a haven for the dregs of society, was destroyed. Although none of Molly's customers expected it, the police decided to investigate. The upshot was that Ahmed Ranji, wealthy restaurant entrepreneur, was arrested for arson.

The court case made the headlines, not least because of the extraordinary array of witnesses for the prosecution. Organized by the Reverend Rick Rattenbury, known as Rick the Revolution in some quarters, citizens of cardboard city came furiously forward in all their unembarrassed scruffiness to testify to what they had seen, namely a gang of hooded thugs, egged on by Councillor Ranji, torching the shed. He seemed not to care if he was recognized, believing himself above the law.

The trial was sensational in many ways. The *Daily Mirror* came up with the headline: *TRAMPS HAVE THEIR DAY IN COURT.* It turned out that some of those who slept near the shed, encased in cardboard, had remarkable tales to tell. Principal among them was Geoffrey Ainger, a one-time detective chief inspector whose career, health, marriage and reputation had been destroyed by promiscuous sexual adventures.

Although a wreck of the man he had once been, Ainger still had some fire in his belly. Refusing money to buy himself new clothes for his court appearance, he stood in the witness box in a tatty old suit, scuffed shoes and a worn out shirt that had lost its collar. 'Why are you here?' asked prosecuting council. The response silenced the muttering that was going on in the public gallery.

'I've made a bloody mess of my life' said the ex-policeman. 'I stood on Hungerford Bridge one night, ready to end it all. Then an old girl in a dirty mac with odd shoes on her feet came up beside me and said for me not to do it. She said to come under the bridge and get some help from Molly. I ended up in the hut eating baked beans and listening to Molly telling me the hard-luck stories of some of those tucked away in cardboard boxes outside her place. That woman saved my life.'

'Whoever torched the hut', said Ainger, 'deserves to burn in the fires of hell. I saw who was responsible. I'd just been down the embankment gardens for a pee behind a statue and came back to see the defendant sending his gangsters in to fire the shed. They kicked a few of the rough sleepers out of the way. Like me, two of those who got kicked are going to testify to see that justice is done.' Ainger paused, as if embarrassed by his own vehemence after years of keeping a low profile, then added, 'I used to try and bring justice to our society but messed up. It's good to have an opportunity to make amends.'

The police federation arranged a public appeal through the *Daily Mail* to restore the shed. It was superior to the old one both in size and appearance and looked a shade incongruous tucked under the bridge. The money raised made possible the provision of a supply of blankets for the rough sleepers. 'Well', exclaimed Molly, 'I'm moving up in the world!'

But Molly declined to restore her name over the door of the new place. There simply appeared, boldly painted in red in capital letters: THE SHED. 'It's not just my place', she told Rick the Revolution. Gesturing to the flotsam and jetsam of society sitting around outside, she fiercely declared: 'It's their place too.'

Politics

*First, they came for the communists, and
I did not speak out because I was not a
communist. Then they came for the socialists,
and I did not speak out because I was not
a socialist. Then they came for the trade
unionists, and I did not speak out because I
was not a trade unionist. Then they came for
the Jews, and I did not speak out because I
was not a Jew. Then they came for me, and
there was no one left to speak out for me.*

Pastor Martin Niemöller

*The most potent and forcible cause of the
destruction was that Rome was afflicted by
the sanguinary quarrels of its nobles and
people.*

Edward Gibbon
Decline and Fall of the Roman Empire

*The sheer size and intricacy of modern
government conspire to thwart all
brisk pretensions to set sensationally
new directions. In the first hours of the
Eisenhower administration, the White House
struggled with no great issue affecting the
destiny of freedom or the welfare of a nation.
The greater part of that memorable day was
spent in trying to unscramble the White
House office switch board.*

Emmett John Hughes

The journalist Henry Mencken on President
Calvin Coolidge:

*He don't say much, but when he does,
he don't say much.*

*Members of Parliament are the blind leading
people who can see.*

G K Chesterton

CHARLOTTE
MAKES A MOVE

Roedean School is a distinguished public boarding school for girls which has produced many women of distinction. It was founded in 1885 near Brighton in Sussex. Pimlico School is a purpose-built showpiece mixed comprehensive established in the centre of London in 1970 by the Inner London Education Authority. Music is a particular strength.

'You cannot be serious!' exclaimed Harold Wiltshire, addressing his teenage daughter Charlotte. It was a statement he had made many times of late. 'She's impossible', he complained to his wife as the girl he had called his little princess in her infancy and childhood had turned into an adolescent firebrand. 'She's like you. She has a mind of her own', came the reply.

'You cannot possibly, under any circumstances whatsoever, be serious', insisted Charlotte's father. 'With the results you have just got, you must return to Roedean for your A levels. I want to see you get a place at Cambridge,' 'What about what I want?' responded his daughter. 'You're not old enough to know what's best for you', insisted her father.

Harold Wiltshire, retired from the army with the rank of Lieutenant Colonel, was accustomed to getting what he wanted. He cared not at all about what other people thought. 'I can't be bothered with anybody who won't cry at my funeral', was one of his favourite utterances. His wife, *who* still cared for him, always offered the same sad reply: 'I know people who will cheer.'

Harold was a big man physically, although his size was as nothing compared to his ego. He was a caricature of a military man. Tall, sturdily built and straight-backed, he had a bristling moustache above firm, some would say petulant, lips. He had been accused by his daughter in one of her more daring moods of addressing everybody, including her, as if they were a public meeting.

The Lieutenant Colonel's petulance overflowed as Charlotte stood her ground. 'I am not spending another two years as a boarder at Roedean. It's full of girls with double-barrelled names who think they are God's gift to the human race and know that daddy will pay up to fix any trouble they get into. I've had enough of Roedean. I want to meet some real members of the human race ...' She paused, then added, provocatively, '... including some boys.'

'God help us, it's sex you're after, is it?' responded

her father, his angry face even more puce than when he had had too many double whiskies at the Carlton Club in St James's Street. He had joined because he had been told it was the club to belong to if you wanted to meet leading figures in the Conservative Party. After the army, politics beckoned. He had been short-listed once for a safe Conservative seat but had alarmed the interviewing panel by the extremity of his opinions when the subject of immigration came up. 'It's time', he said, 'some of these little black men went back where they came from. Lots of people think that but are afraid to say so. Me, I'm never afraid of saying things that upset the let-'em-all-in mob. Had an African johnny in my battalion once. Couldn't take a joke. Complained when the other men made monkey noises when he arrived on parade each morning. No sense of humour. Not an Englishman, y'see. He had to go.'

In the end Harold had settled for a part-time appointment as an advisor on army recruitment at the Ministry of Defence. He had hoped for something more prestigious. 'It's because I got an O, not a K', he complained to James Jenkins, the barman at the club. He was on his third double whisky at the time and always became loquacious when tanked up. James was used to hearing his tales. 'I tell you, my friend', he continued, 'if I was *Sir* Harold, businesses would want me on their stationery as a board member.'

Charlotte despised her father. Something Jimmy Porter said about his father-in-law in the play *Look Back in Anger* came to mind. The outrageous star of John Osborne's seminal play, he told his wife's father that he was left over from a previous era and couldn't understand why, for people like him, the sun wasn't shining any more. Charlotte regarded her father as a man living in the past, with opinions that had no place in the modern world.

'I'll be eighteen by the end of next year and know for sure what I want to do. I want to get enrolled for the sixth form at Pimlico School for September', Charlotte announced to her parents. 'If you don't let me', she declared loudly, as if addressing a public meeting, 'I will just drop out and take to the streets.'

'Well', said her mother, 'Pimlico is only a bus ride away from here in Belgravia, which would be quite convenient.' But, in a spirit of genuine inquiry, she asked whether the state comprehensive at Pimlico, purpose built at great expense, wasn't the school that had been in the papers for appointing security guards to patrol the corridors to keep order. Charlotte gave a deep chuckle. 'Mother', she said, 'don't tell me you've been reading the *Daily Mirror*. Emily says the gutter press camped outside the school for days when that story was on the go. Actually, the security guards were for protecting the place from intruders. The school is quite famous for its orchestra and thieves had just waltzed in one day and stolen a load of valuable instruments. It was in the papers.'

Charlotte's parents discussed their daughter's request for their support, and her threat to drop out if it was not forthcoming. 'I'll drop her out with my swagger stick if she doesn't come to her senses', threatened her father. 'Harold, the days when the law allowed that sort of thing are gone' said his wife, 'Charlotte is a young woman now. Don't you know your daughter? She's quite capable of walking out on us if you try to bully her.'

The girl had in fact already walked out of the house after dinner, saying she was going to see her friend Emily, whom she had known way back before being sentenced to five years at Roedean. Emily had been at Pimlico for five years and was about to enter the sixth form. The two girls had kept in touch over the years.

Emily and Charlotte chatted away, getting up to date. They did so in Emily's bedroom which Charlotte's father would have regarded as a den of iniquity. Mick Jagger posters covered two walls. 'We weren't allowed pop star posters at Roedean,' said Charlotte, 'Miss Holland said they were all into drugs and, as she put it' – Charlotte imitated the voice of the headmistress – 'their influence on you gels is not to be tolerated' Emily said, 'I bet she doesn't know that Mick Jagger went to university.

He was at the LSE reading economics. He dropped out when the Rolling Stones started to make the news. Mick always claimed that he gave up studying economics when his own economic situation took off. The LSE kept his place open for him for a couple of years in case he decided to return.'

Charlotte explained that, when she had told her father she wanted to attend Pimlico sixth form, he said she couldn't be serious, but she thought her mother could talk him round. 'With all his army bluster, he's not actually very bright. Mum will fix it. She is very clever at persuading him that what she wants him to do was his idea all along. She says all husbands are like that.'

Chatting to members in the bar at the Carlton Club, Harold let on that his daughter Charlotte was doing very well at Pimlico School. 'I thought she was at Roedean', said Julian Andrews, a fund manager at a merchant bank. 'Yes, she was', replied Harold, 'but we decided it was time she left a girls' public school and mixed with some ordinary youngsters.' 'Hum', said Julian, 'but aren't there boys at Pimlico? That'll be a new world for Charlotte. Sex is all they think about at her age. I bet you hope your daughter doesn't get pregnant.' Harold turned to the bar. 'Top me up again, James', said Harold, with a slightly nervous tremor in his voice.

How The Young See Others

My name is Christopher. I am a boy. I don't fight. The colour of my hair is brown. I like my school and I like my teacher. I like doing PE and I love Susan. She is very, very lovely. And I am not tall.

Christopher

Some people have longer arms than others. It depends where their sleeves end.

Tina Firth

A thirteen-year-old girl wrote a poem about her grandma which ended like this:

I bent forward and kissed her wrinkled cheek.
It was like kissing clay,
All cold and soft.
I took a deep breath and smelt
Mint humbugs and golden fudges.
I felt saddened by the way she moved,
Like a clock winding down.

Gail Bloomfield

A class in their early teens was asked to write about what made people great. One girl of independent mind did not write about characters the class had been studying:

Once there was a woman who had done a big washing and hung it on the line. The line broke and let it all down in the mud, but she did not say a word, only did it all over again. This time she spread it on the grass where it could not fall but a dog with dirty feet ran all over it. All she said was: 'Ain't it queer he didn't miss nothing.' That was true greatness. But it's only people who have done the washing that understand.

Louise Jenkins

STICKY WICKET

James Baker, seventeen, sat upstairs, at the front, on the number 74 bus, his cricket bag at his feet, and whispered a short prayer: 'Please God, let it rain.' He had a very informal relationship with God and quite often chatted up the maker of all things visible and invisible when he needed a bit of help. When Jake, James's close friend, tried to wind him up over his perception of him upstairs, as he put it, being a sort of divine supermarket manager, standing by to fulfil customers' orders, James just smiled knowingly.

God had recently come to his aid when he had been struggling to remember the *Rectitudines* for his A level history mock at Sutton Grammar School. That mediaeval document set out the responsibilities of everyone living on a twelfth century manorial estate. The *Rectitudines Singularum Personarum* spelled out the duties of every single person from the villein working the land to the lord of the manor and his many officials. Struggling to remember the details, James had looked up into the sky out of his open bedroom window. Leaning on the sill, he cried out for help. Dropping his gaze, he saw the washing on the line in the back garden. His spirits lifted. 'Thank you God', he said.

James put up a piece of string across his bedroom so that it hung at eye level. He pegged scraps of paper on it, each bearing one of the *Rectitudines.* Every night, on going to bed, he looked at his historical washing. He ended up able to recite the *Rectitudines Singularum Personarum* like nobody else in his history set.

Sitting on the bus on the way to play for the school in the southern counties schools cricket finals, James was worried. After a week of baking July sunshine, the wicket at the Oval would be extremely hard. That would just suit Pickering, the Maidstone Grammar School paceman, a tall, aggressive bowler with a thirty yard run up who terrified opposition batsmen and who had demolished Sutton's top order last season. James was also an opening bowler and quite fast, but he was no paceman. He was a swing bowler and a seamer. Moving the ball off the seam was easier on a moist wicket, hence James's request to God, who had sorted out his history swotting.

James thought the Almighty was very likely a cricket enthusiast. Well, the game had more rules than the ten commandments and had to do with what you believed. Trevor Durston, the Sutton cricket coach, taught that believing in yourself was the key to success in any sport. And didn't Jesus say: 'All things are possible to those who believe'? And: 'Ask and it will be given to you'? So, mused James, a wet afternoon wasn't much to ask.

As the bus rumbled through the south London streets on its way from Charing Cross, where James had got off the train, towards the Oval Cricket Ground, he looked out of the window into the sky, hoping for some grey clouds. But the azure blue was cloudless and his heart sank. 'Please God', he whispered, 'send down some rain. If you do, I'll be more helpful at home. I know I promised that before when I wanted you to get that girl to like me, but I really mean it this time. Please, some rain.'

The bus collected supporters from both schools as it neared the Oval. Others streamed out of the underground station nearby. Excited chatter filled the air as if a flock of noisy birds was whirling overhead. James saw staff arriving in cars and taxis. He spotted Pickering towering over a group from Maidstone as they got off a line of coaches. He looked sickeningly confident.

Jake waved to James from one of the Sutton coaches pulling in. James preferred to travel alone, free of all the fooling about on a coach that would have unnerved him. The occasion was too big for that. James knew that staff on the coaches would be unable to maintain control on a finals day like this one. Some of the fifth formers who were always making trouble in school would have smuggled cans of beer on board. God help the boys who were natural victims.

As if to confirm his suspicions, James saw a small boy named Bennett in the third year, who was often the subject of ragging, scramble off a coach without his shoes. The teacher in charge was Shouty Smith, so called because he was always yelling at his classes to shut up. He was raging at boys who were tossing Bennett's footwear about. James turned his head away. 'I can do without that', he told himself, 'I've got to keep my mind on outperforming Pickering today.'

Sutton won the toss and their two openers went in to bat at eleven o'clock. Pickering ripped out the stumps of both of them in his first two overs. A trail of destruction was halted by Sutton's numbers three and four, who put on 64 between them before both fell to Pickering in his second spell.

Two knowledgable followers of Surrey County Cricket Club, whose home ground was the Oval, noticed that the Surrey coach was watching proceedings closely. 'He's come to see that Pickering boy', said one. 'Yes', said his companion, 'there's no schoolboy bowler to match him. He'll be playing for Surrey one day.'

After two hours, with lunch approaching, James was at the wicket, batting at number ten. He and the Sutton number eleven obstinately refused to go quietly. They stonewalled everything and even managed four singles. The Maidstone captain was furious so he brought Pickering back on for a final spell. 'Get one of these two buggers out', he was told. He added: 'I don't care how you do it!'

James's fellow batsman, Phil Kelly by name, was a spin bowler of small stature. Pickering hurled down a bouncer that skipped off the edge of his bat. 'Yes', shouted James, and hurtled down the pitch. Pickering stepped across his path and brought him down so that he was run out. 'You're a cheating bastard', said James. 'Yea', sneered Pickering, 'we aim to win this match. You've no chance.' The Sutton innings closed at one o'clock with 103 runs on the board. Pickering had taken 5 for 36. One of the knowledgeable observers said, 'Sutton have no bowler to beat that.'

'The game's over', said Jack Henry, the Sutton captain, who had made just 28 runs batting at number three. 'Not yet, it isn't', muttered James Baker as he looked out from the pavilion to the darkening sky. A few minutes later, rain began to fall on the uncovered wicket.

The afternoon's play was delayed but the rain eased off. By 2.30 it had stopped and the sun had come out again. As the Sutton team trotted on to the field, Jack Henry called James Baker and Phil Kelly to him. He said, 'You may have thought the game was all over, but we've caught them on a sticky wicket. Just right for you, Phil, with your leg breaks. And it will swing in the air in this humid atmosphere and move off the seam with the pitch nice and wet. Ideal for you, James. Somebody up there must be looking after you.'

As James measured his fifteen yard run up, he chatted to the God in whom he profoundly believed. 'Thank you', he whispered, 'but don't let the wicket dry out. We need it to stay sticky.' He paused and added, 'Sorry. I guess you know what you're doing.' He turned and faced the batsman, smiling in the knowledge that nobody stood a chance facing him and God working together.

And so it proved. By the time of the tea break at 4.30, James and Phil had taken two wickets each and Maidstone were 43 for four. But, by then, the sun had been blazing down for some time and the wicket was drying rapidly. Maidstone's middle batsmen were settling in and boundaries were beginning to flow. 'Come on', whispered James, looking skywards as he headed for tea, 'Let's have another shower or two'. As rainfall hammered the pavilion roof during tea, the Maidstone captain grumbled to his players, 'It's like there's someone in the Sutton team who manages the weather. I bet the sun will come out again in a minute.' And, of course, it did, keeping the wicket the way the bowlers wanted it.

Maidstone's remaining batsmen only made 36 as

Jimmy picked four of them off and Phil the other two. With figures of 6 for 32, James was the hero of the hour. In school assembly on Monday morning, he was presented with the match ball as a momento of his performance.

At morning break, James sat quietly in the corner of the prefects' room and addressed God. 'Thanks for that wet afternoon on Saturday', he said, 'that was great. Now, about my application for a place at Oxford.'

Teenagers

*A teacher told me that, if I wore pink socks
to school, I wouldn't be able to concentrate
on my Latin. We were ticked off for leaving
greasy chip papers around and were told
that, if we did that sort of thing, we would
sleep with so many blokes. If they'd just said
it was nasty to leave greasy papers around,
we'd have taken some notice.*

Helen MacRae

The father of a thirteen-year-old boy wrote to
Chatham House School about his son:

*Please give your permission for Edward
Heath to attend Cave's Cafe for his dinner
as we find that school dinners do not agree
with him.*

Marian Evans

*Returning to school after a spell in hospital,
a fourteen-year-old boy was complimented
by his headmaster on his new, traditional
hair style. The boy explained: 'Sister was
combing my hair in the normal way and I
was shouting at her, but I had only just come
round from the anaesthetic so I couldn't do
anything to stop her.'*

Anon

*On my sixteenth birthday, I got a ton of
sand to make a jumping pit in the field
behind our house.*

Mary Peters

Report to a school by a local authority's
educational psychologist after referring a
highly disruptive teenage girl for advice:

*Judicious permissiveness and self-expression
opportunities, with guided and supported
channelization of released drives, would help.*

Michael Watt

NAPOLEON SMITH
AND THE VULTURE

Napoleon Smith had been given his first name by parents who wanted their son to be noticed, despite his being one of the mighty army of Smiths in the world. His Napoleonic moniker made him the butt of many jokes at school. When, at the age of fourteen, he turned up with his arm in plaster after falling off his bike on an icy street during his paper round, Jake Johnson made up a rhyme that was called after him as he went about the school:

Napoleon's a proper laugh,
He's gone and broke his boney part.

Napoleon hated Jake, who made his life a misery, stealing his books, pushing him about in the school corridors and deflating the tyres of his bike in the school cycle sheds. Napoleon's cleverness in class, and habit of always getting his homework in on time, irked his persecutor who, along with a slim, almost skeletal frame, had an aquiline nose that he thrust forwards when speaking. Some said he resembled a vulture, but not to his face. Napoleon resolved to have his revenge one day.

Napoleon's school career was highly successful. He went on to graduate in business studies and took a post at a bank in a London suburb. Highly intelligent, always punctual and immaculate in his dress, with an appetite for hard work, he was seen as a man with a great future ahead of him. By the age of thirty-two, Napoleon Smith was number two at the bank and in charge when the manager took his holidays. One morning, a customer named Johnson with an account at the bank asked to see the manager. So it was that Napoleon Smith and Jake Johnson came face to face once more.

Jake did not recognize Napoleon. The relaxed and confident man before him bore little likeness to the boy he remembered as a weedy swot whom he had pushed around and persecuted. But Napoleon recognized his visitor. Although his body had filled out, and his face become rotund and bright red from the onset of alcoholism, the vulture-like nose was unmistakable.

'So, Mr Johnson', said Napoleon, 'how may the bank be of help to you?' 'Well', said his visitor, 'I need an overdraft to tide me over for a few months while some of my business dealings come good.' 'I see', responded Napoleon, 'and what dealings are they?' 'What does that matter?' Jake irritably replied, 'They're this and that. You know. I've got all sorts of interests.'

'Well', said Napoleon, 'if the bank is to lend you money, we like to have some idea of what it's for. It's what we call responsible lending.' He laid a strong emphasis on the penultimate word. 'After all', he went on, laughing as he did so, 'we wouldn't want to be caught out financing a criminal activity.'

Jake's red face became positively scarlet. 'Who are you calling a criminal?' he exclaimed, 'Some of my best friends are coppers.' I bet they are, thought Napoleon to himself, especially those to whom you have bunged a few readies from time to time. Vulture Johnson, as Jake was known among the local criminal fraternity, liked to keep the police from investigating some of his activities too closely.

Napoleon was puzzled that an allegedly wealthy crook should want a bank overdraft. He was deeply suspicious, but decided to play along with Jake and see where it led. 'I am required to ask you', he said, 'how much you want, and for how long, and for what purpose.' Jake explained that his account at the bank was for what he called domestic purposes. 'Me big money's not in this country. Good God, no. I wouldn't want the tax man to get his hands on it.'

Jake still hadn't explained what he wanted an overdraft for and Napoleon realized he wasn't going to say. He discerned that his visitor had some nefarious purpose in coming. He decided to call a halt to proceedings. He said: 'I'm sorry, Mr Johnson, I can't allow you to overdraw your account.' The Vulture was incredulous. 'Why the hell not?', he asked. 'You know', he went on, with a threatening note in his voice, 'people don't usually say no to me.' 'I'm sure they don't', came the reply, 'but I'm going to because, to be frank, I'm suspicious. You won't answer my questions.'

The Vulture's anger was tangible. 'Answer your questions? People don't question me. I question them. And if they don't give the right answers, God help them.' He rose to his feet and stormed to the door. Opening it wide, he swept his arm towards the long counter in the main lobby of the bank and the startled staff behind it. Malvolio-like, he declared, 'I'll be revenged on the lot of you', and stormed out.

Detective Chief Inspector Blakemore was mystified by the murder of a young woman, Kate Evans, who appeared to have been knifed on the way home from work. Her body lay in a ditch which ran beside the local railway track. She had not been molested and her handbag, with all its contents intact, including her purse and credit cards, lay nearby. The DCI addressed his team. He sighed as he said: 'A murder on our patch will have the nationals making big headlines.'

Blakemore gave instructions for close examination of the site where the girl's body had been found; for his DI to find out the girl's usual route home from work and take some uniformed men to explore it; for the most experienced woman on his team to visit the girl's parents. 'We know the deceased, Kate Evans, shared a flat with another girl so DS Hunt will come with me to explore that avenue', said Blakemore. 'We must all jump to it because the press will be on to this in no time.'

It turned out that the girl with whom Kate Evans lived, Sharon Grace by name, worked with her at a local bank. The death of her friend and colleague broke her in pieces. Between her tears she explained that Kate had no enemies. 'She was just an ordinary girl, like me', she said, 'with absolutely nothing in her life that might make someone want to kill her. We were a couple of nobodies. We didn't even have steady boyfriends'.

Blakemore gave a press conference which led to some sensational tabloid headlines. He decided to go on local television. He was fully open in answering questions, making it plain that the police were baffled. A picture of Kate Evans appeared on the screen.

When Napoleon arrived home, his wife said: 'One of your girls at the bank had her picture on TV – the one who approached me at the church garden party in the summer to tell me what a nice man you were to work for. She's been murdered on her way home from the bank. Who on earth would want to kill her?' Napoleon furiously hurled his briefcase across the kitchen where his wife was preparing dinner. 'Damn him', he shouted. 'It's Johnson getting his own back. He said he'd have his revenge. That Vulture has taken his anger out on an innocent girl.'

At the police station, he explained his suspicions to Blakemore, who had had several run-ins with Jake Johnson before but had never been able to nail him. The DCI said, 'This is very interesting. We've been watching Johnson for some time. One of our informants in the criminal fraternity has told us that he's been lining things up for a bank robbery. He and his gang have been visiting banks on some pretext or other in order to choose one that would be easy to hold up on a quiet day of the week.'

The Vulture's downfall was brought about by his arrogance. Following Kate Evans from the bank as she made her homeward journey, he jumped her as she left the road to walk along the footpath high above a railway track. One gloved hand covered her mouth while the other thrust a knife into her back. He threw her inert body down the railway bank so that it rolled into a ditch below. Taking off his gloves and stuffing them in his pocket, he rubbed his hands together with satisfaction. That would teach a lesson to that bank manager who had dared to challenge him. Picking up the girl's bag, he tossed it down after her.

But for Napoleon's visit to the police, Blakemore might never have connected Jake Johnson with Kate Evans' murder. Once the fingerprints on her handbag had been checked against police records, they had the killer, as they say, bang to rights. 'Just take note of this', said the DCI to a couple of newcomers to his team, 'It's often the little things that are important in detective work. The Vulture made one small mistake. With any luck, he'll be thinking about that for the next twenty years inside.'

Be Careful What You Say

When I use a word, it means whatever I choose it to mean.

> Humpty Dumpty in 'Through the Looking Glass', Lewis Carroll

I don't always know what I'm talking about, but I know I'm right.

> Mohammad Ali to Harry Carpenter

In classical times, when Cicero had finished speaking, the people said 'How well he spoke', but when Demosthenes spoke they said, 'Let us march!'

> Adlai Stevenson

You are what you do, not what you say you will do.

> Carl Jung

Silence is not golden; silence is chicken.

Ed Koch, Mayor of Chicago

Alec Bedser's mother, asked on BBC Radio 4 whether she was proud of her son when he skittled the Australian batsmen, replied, 'I thought that's what he was supposed to do.'

For one word, a man is often deemed to be wise; for one word deemed to be foolish.

Confucius

Telling lies to the young is wrong.
Proving to them that lies are true is wrong.
Telling them that God's in his heaven
and all's well with the world is wrong.

Yevgeny Yuvteshenko

WE NEED TO TALK

In the first week of April in 1989, my education column in the Daily Telegraph was devoted to the decline of conversation in the home. The article, published twenty-five years ago, which appears below, identified a problem that persists for those working in schools.

Speaking at a meeting in London recently, Norris McWhirter, Chairman of the Freedom Association, reported the result of a survey showing how much time parents spend talking to each other in their homes. The appalling statistic was 22 minutes a week.

Never mind which social group was surveyed. Practising teachers know that, today, large numbers of parents, from all walks of life, have a communication problem. Exchanges between them, and conversations with their children, are snatched during television advertisements.

Anyone who thinks violence is the only phenomenon attributable to television does not know what is going on. Ed Murrow was right when he described the glowing picture in the corner as chewing gum for the eyes. The inability of young people to string together a coherent series of sentences is down to the fact that no-one talks at home any more.

If you think that is an exaggeration, have a word with the next teacher you meet who works with infants. Going about the country, I get the same message everywhere from those responsible for handling reception classes in schools. The children being received are less articulate than used to be the case. As a society, we are moving backwards, not forwards, in producing citizens capable of conversing.

Infant school teachers also complain that those toddling into the class-room these days have not been prepared by parents to start school, as once was the case. They cannot dress themselves, put on their own shoes or sit still.

As well as being unable to communicate or look after themselves, many children cannot count to six before the teaching profession gets to work on them. Mind you, we should not be too surprised: innumeracy is rife throughout our society. Being no good at maths is regarded as socially acceptable.

The latest example of this comes with Lord Elton's report on discipline in schools. What his lordship has made of the information placed before him shows that interpreting statistics is not one of his strengths.

A survey commissioned by his committee discovered that 1.7 per cent of teachers were victims of physical aggression in the classroom in one particular week in September last year. In a teaching force of 400,000 that amounts to more than 6,000 teachers assaulted. From this degree of violence in just one week, Lord Elton draws the astonishing conclusion that attacks on teachers are of no significant dimensions. In a school year of 40 weeks the scale of the problem is deeply disturbing.

Lord Elton and his committee really ought to have been able to work that out for themselves by looking at the statistics that were in front of them. Clearly, it was a grave omission that membership of the committee was not made conditional upon candidates passing a simple maths test.

Seeing that the mathematical competence of the great and good has been demonstrated to be wanting, it is all the more important that we get things right in schools with the next generation. National testing has not come too soon. Children ought to be tested at the start of their infant education. Only by such means will it be possible to judge what schools achieve, or fail to achieve.

No normal child should be admitted to school unless capable of passing some simple tests, such as counting to six and knowing the alphabet. Some schools already make such demands. How about making it a national requirement? It would bring dilatory parents face to face with their responsibilities, and compel them to talk to their children.

John Donne

Born in London in 1572, Donne had a keen brain and a romantic disposition. He entered the priesthood in 1614 at the age of 42 after an adventurous life as a lawyer, a soldier and an MP. Dean of St Paul's Cathedral from 1621, he gained a reputation as a great preacher, writer and poet. Living at a time of religious and political turmoil, he managed to keep his head when others were losing theirs.

On churchgoers hearing a funeral bell:

Perchance he for whom the bell tolls may be so ill that he knows not it tolls for him. No man is an island entire of itself. If a clod be washed away by the sea, it is the less, as well as if a manor of thy friends or thine own were. Any man's death diminishes me because I am involved in mankind. And therefore never send to know for whom the bell tolls. It tolls for thee.

Preaching at St Paul's at Easter on the miraculous:

There is nothing that God has established in a constant course of nature, and which therefore is done every day, but would seem a miracle, if it were done but once. The standing still of the sun in the time of Joshua was not of itself so wonderful as the daily motion of the sun, but the daily doing takes off the admiration.

Extract from poem to his wife entitled 'The Anniversarie':

All other things to their destruction draw,
Only our love hath no decay;
This no tomorrow hath, nor yesterday,
But truly keeps his first, last, everlasting day.

MY FATHER JUDAH

Judah Dawson was one of thirteen children fathered by Isaac Davidson, an impoverished Jew of the diaspora, the dispersion. Isaac came to England some time in the nineteenth century. He attenuated his name to Dawson for reasons unknown and married Mary O'Connell, a girl who had fled a life of grinding poverty in Ireland. How the two met is not known but they raised their family in the East End of London.

Born in 1900, Judah grew up a street urchin within the sound of Bow Bells. In adulthood, his speech was a mixture of cockney slang and yiddisher from his Jewish heritage. On the one hand, he called his socks his almond rocks and on the other he described anyone he didn't like as a schmuk.

Chasing round the streets of the East End as a boy, he and his mates used to run into the main road and jump on the backs of lorries for a free ride. One day Judah fell off under the wheels of a tram and lost most of one foot.

Not long after the outbreak of war in 1939, with a German invasion seemingly imminent, my father abandoned the name Judah and called himself Richard. When asked why, he said: 'We're not going to no concentrated camp.'

My father's Jewish roots were most clearly exposed when the extended family was gathered on special occasions. Then it was that Dick Dawson's skill as a teller of Jewish jokes was celebrated.

Someone would demand that he told the tale of Yossel and Schmulick. I can hear his voice now as he regaled the company.

Yossel and Schmulick are sitting in the synagogue on the Sabbath. While the rabbi reads from the holy scroll, Schmulick shuffles his feet and groans. Afterwards, Yossel asks, 'For why were you shuffling your feet?' Schmulick explains that his shoes are too tight and are crippling him. 'Then why don't you get some shoes that fit?' exclaims Yossel. 'Well,' replies Schmulick, 'it's like this. My son has dropped out of university; my daughter, would you believe, wants to marry a goy, a gentile; the roof of my house leaks; my business is failing and my wife never stops nagging me. My whole life is a disaster. But when I get home from my day's work and take my shoes off, for a few moments, I feel wonderful.'

In adulthood, he who had been Judah and was now known as Dickie Dawson worked nights at the *Daily Express* in Fleet Street, tying up packs of newspapers as they rolled off the presses and loading them into vans for distribution to newsagents across the country. If any part of the process of writing, typesetting, printing, packing and distributing the paper so that copies were on newsagents' doorsteps by first light failed, the editor would go berserk.

This gave the print unions enormous power. The mightiest of them was the National Society of Operative Printers and Assistants, the Natsopas. Dickie Dawson was father of the chapel in the *Daily Express* warehouse. It was not a religious appointment. He was shop steward. Back in the 1950s, Fleet Street shop stewards were more powerful than the newspaper owners, who lived in fear of losing a day's sales.

As a hard-up university student, I got a job wheeling huge photographic plates up and down Fleet Street on a trolley. This was only possible because my father contrived to get me a Natsopas union ticket, which opened an Aladdin's cave of opportunities in the newspaper industry.

I was interviewed for the job by Tom Jago, father of the chapel at my proposed place of work. He said, 'Right, we'll take you on. I'll tell the management.' On my first morning he said, 'Take your time. Don't go rushing about. You're covering a man on leave and he don't want to get back and find you've made his job hard work.'

My father had a keen intelligence and saw what was going to happen to the newspaper industry. It operated in a world of its own, fatally believing itself insulated from forces at work in the world at large.

A pub at the bottom of Fleet Street stayed open all night to give workers some relief from the frantic activity of newspaper production. It also enabled reporters to check their stories with others of their kind. The enclosed world of Fleet Street even had its own church. St Bride's is still known as the printers' church and has a chapel devoted to journalists killed reporting wars across the globe.

My father predicted the flight of the press from Fleet Street. He realised that the old way of producing newspapers, with compositors setting the type for fixing to metal plates laid on great rollers, would not continue. The arrival of computers and desk-top publishing, which was simpler, quicker and cheaper, was imminent.

My father also predicted that the changes that were coming would break the power of the great print unions. He explained that every man at the *Daily Express* had a cover man in case of illness.

But the union negotiators had succeeded in persuading the bosses that every cover man should get full pay even if he didn't have to come in. 'We couldn't believe it when the bosses said yes to that', said my father. 'They're scared of us. But we have been fools too. We know the bosses are discussing moving out of Fleet Street, but we tell ourselves they wouldn't dare.'

Like many ordinary working men in his time, Dick Dawson was a compulsive gambler. My mother said he was very interested in sick horses, but didn't know they were sick when he bet on them. When it was time for the Derby, he got all his racing books out and checked the pedigree and racing record of each horse. In due course, he would confidently announce that such-and-such a horse was bound to win. When subsequently asked why his prediction had been wrong, he would say that the ground was too soft or the horse had a bad draw or the wrong jockey was on him.

Dick Dawson looked just like the American film star James Cagney. If a Cagney film was on at our local cinema, he insisted on taking us to see it. When we were coming out at the end, people would look at my dad and do a double take. He loved that.

He was envious of my spending two years in the military when I was called up for National Service at eighteen. My dad, with his crippled foot, thought square bashing and being shouted at by drill corporals sounded great fun. On leave at the end of recruit training, I related how I had once failed to swing my arms sufficiently when marching. An NCO, bringing his face close up to mine, bawled: 'If you don't get those arms moving, airman, I'll pull one of 'em off and beat your bloody head in with the soggy end.' Being just out of the sixth form and rather full of myself after getting good A Level results, I felt like saying: 'Well my good man, my head certainly would be bloody if you did that', but I wisely declined. Father wished he could have had such an experience. For him, the grass was greener on the side of the street where men with two feet marched.

My father died at 62 of lung cancer. Like many working class men of his time, he was a chain smoker. I was at his bedside when he died at home, the hospital surgeons having opened him up, shaken their heads in despair, sewn him up again and sent him home to die. His lungs were a labyrinth of nicotine. He was spewing up a thick stream of the stuff as he breathed his last.

You could say that my dad had the last laugh with the bookies. Three weeks before he died, he placed £10 on a horse called Kilmore for the Grand National, which was five weeks away. Because he placed the bet so long in advance, he got odds of ten to one. By the time of the race, Kilmore was second favourite at six to four. When it won, my widowed mother received a hundred pounds from dad's bookmaker. She said, 'That's nice. It's the most money I've ever had off him from his gambling. God bless the old sod.' And so said all of us who knew and loved him.

Holocaust Haiku

Spring in the death camp
Was a dark time for us Jews
Gas ovens roaring

Summer was as bad
Heavy was the curse on us
Each day that season

So that was Auschwitz
In our hearts always winter
Hate still haunts Hebrews

UNFORGETTABLE

In the USA, they say that everyone knows where they were when President Kennedy was assassinated. He had just been hugely encouraged by his reception in Dallas, but disaster struck just when things were going well. Some who perished when the *Titanic* hit an iceberg had been dining sumptuously immediately before; others, of humbler status, accommodated in the steerage section of the ship, were leaving poverty behind and looking forward to a new and better life the other side of the Atlantic. Sometimes, the memorable events in life are those when our dreams are realized. But, as with the bullet that blew the top of Jack Kennedy's head off, and the sinking of the *Titanic*, which was believed to be unsinkable, when a time of promise is suddenly overwhelmed by disaster, the event is doubly memorable. The following record of events has to do with that.

Autumn 1951. Trees on the high ground overlooking RAF Credenhill, near Hereford, were dressed in a breathtaking range of browns and golds. Oh, to be in England now that autumn's here. But my destiny was to leave these gloriously colourful scenes for the Egyptian desert.

Just out of the grammar school sixth form, where keeping a balance between rugby, cricket and the debating society on the one hand and GCE Advanced Levels on the other, tested my priorities, the brave new world of National Service in the RAF looked inviting. It was to present me with the most devastatingly memorable experience of my life; one that has left a permanent imprint on my beliefs.

Recruit training at Credenhill, known colloquially as square-bashing, was an astonishing experience. Freddie Truman, a frighteningly fast bowler from Yorkshire, who had been denied postponement of his National Service despite having been selected to play for England in the West Indies, sat on the end of his bed the first night and, at great length, swore at the MoD. It made me realize my unpreparedness for life in the real world – many of the swear words were unknown to me. Someone laid a bet, challenging his fellow recruits to tip Freddie out of bed during the night. One chap was prepared to take up the challenge. The rest of us thought he was a fool but, if he was of a mind to avoid National Service by getting bashed up by Fiery Fred and crippled for life, his foolhardiness might do the trick.

After lights out, we peered from behind our blankets to see what would happen. The chap who had taken up the challenge tipped Freddie out of bed and shot out the door, hotly pursued by England's future cricketing star. We waited for the return of the foolhardy fellow who had turned Freddie's bed over. We expected much blood. But chaser and chased returned the best of pals. 'What happened?', we asked. Truman replied, in his tough Yorkshire patois: 'I caught booger, put 'im down and asked 'im what were bloody bet. He said ten quid. We thought a fiver each would be about right, so I didn't bash 'im.' I thought to myself that life in the RAF was going to be an exciting education.

Another dramatic development was imminent. Hoping to avoid spending two years in some uninteresting job in the UK, I was delighted to be selected for flying control. My training was to take place in the control tower at RAF Mauripur near Karachi in Pakistan. I was going to see the world and spend my time with aeroplanes. Hooray!

Flown out from Lyneham with a number of other newcomers to the RAF, we arrived at a tented transit camp at El Hamra, near the Suez Canal. This was at the beginning of the 1950s, just a few years from the time when Sir Anthony Eden decided upon an invasion of Suez by British troops. The atmosphere at El Hamra was tense, with local Arabs taking pot shots at anyone venturing out into the nearby desert. RAF personnel stationed at El Hamra carried arms at all times, even when off duty in the station cinema. Sitting among men with rifles between their knees was something new. It made going to the pictures to see a Doris Day musical a strange experience.

The six of us who were sharing a tent were a motley crew. Harry had the biggest personality. A tall, suave chap with a posh voice, educated at a public school, he had views on everything and loudly expressed them at every opportunity. It was no surprise to learn that he intended to go on the stage. He claimed to have a place at RADA awaiting the completion of his military service.

After breakfast one morning, the six of us were called up over the tannoy to report to the armoury. Equipped with rifles and clips of ammunition, we were to provide the rear guard of a convoy going down the road beside the canal to Ismailia. But as we were climbing aboard the open lorry from which we were to keep a look-out for hostiles, I was told to return my arms and pack my kit ready for departure to Pakistan. While on the whole glad to be moving on, I was a shade disappointed to be denied the chance of desert heroics. The achievements of the desert rats in the war against Hitler had always excited me. I rather liked the idea of being like those who chased Rommel across North Africa. My immaturity was about to be brought home to me.

In what seemed no time at all, and before I had

left the scene, the vehicle in which my breakfast companions had driven off was back. It struggled slowly, grindingly, through the station gate in an advanced state of destruction. There were bullet holes the length of the vehicle, with blood flowing from some of them. Harry and the other four men with whom I had shared a tent and breakfasted were all dead. Harry, with his thespian ambitions, had rather fancied himself as good-looking. He wasn't now. Most of his head had been blown off by a rocket from a bazooka and only the stump of his neck remained. Without thinking what I was doing, I stepped forward to help unload the bodies and ended up with blood on my recently acquired, unblemished desert khaki.

I was not long out of the security of a grammar school in a leafy part of Kent, the garden of England, with little experience of real life. For the first time, I realized that armed conflict was not just an adventure used by film makers to sell their products; it was a heartbreaking business. Like those whose dead bodies I helped unload, I was just eighteen years old and deeply affected. Memorable? Yes, devastatingly so. For many years, I was unable to speak of the never-to-be-forgotten horror witnessed one morning in the sands of Egypt.

Now eighty years of age, that period in my oh-so-young life erupts in my mind when reports of desert conflict appear in the news, not least when one hears of young soldiers being blown up in the sands of Afghanistan. News reports say that some traumatized troops need counselling when they return home. I know just how they feel.

Leaving Auschwitz

We explained that we were Italian Jews who came from Auschwitz and were going through Katowice on the way home. Jews who had survived Auschwitz? The old woman's look mellowed. She took us into a back room, made us sit down, offered us two glasses of real beer, and at once poured forth her story with pride.

She had owned a shop in Berlin, with her husband. They had never liked Hitler, and they had allowed their opinions to leak out. In 1935 her husband had been taken away by the Gestapo. But one has to live and she had continued her business until 1938, when Hitler had made his famous speech on the radio in which he had declared that he wanted to start a war.

Then she had grown angry and had written to him, addressing him personally: 'To Mr Adolf Hitler, Chancellor of the Reich, Berlin.' She advised him strongly not to wage war because too many people would be killed. She pointed out that he would lose because Germany could not win against the whole world; even a child could understand that. She had signed the letter with her name, surname and address. Then she had settled down to wait.

Five days later the brown-shirts arrived. They turned her house upside down and she thought they would beat her up and send her to a concentration camp. Instead, they said she was a stupid old goat and deported her to Katowice.

She had been living, hand to mouth, in the town which was only a few miles from Auschwitz until, as she had foreseen, the Germans lost the war. Then the Polish authorities granted her a licence for a grocery store. So, in the end, she lived in peace, fortified by the thought of how much better the world would be if the rulers of this earth followed her advice.

Primo Levi

BIG DAY AT THE PALACE

In the citation that hangs on the wall in my study at home, signed *Elizabeth R,* Her Majesty describes me as a trusty and well beloved recipient of the dignity and rank of an Officer of the Most Excellent Order of the British Empire.

From time to time, when my wife is inclined to dismiss my opinion on any matter, a situation that occurs with great frequency, I remind her that there is another woman in my life who regards me as her beloved. Sadly, this never affects her poor evaluation of my views, but one learns to be philosophical. How it came about that this writer was appointed an OBE, and what occurred when I stood before our monarch, and subsequently, will now be related.

My wife and two daughters were anxious to arrive early at Buckingham Palace for the investiture because they wanted time to see the royal toilets. We who were to be honoured were taken off to have the procedure awaiting us explained and to advise us how to bow to the Queen and address her. We were told that we would have only one, or at most two, minutes in front of her. She devoted a good deal more time than that to me. Why?

I had spent ten years as headmaster of a purpose-built, Inner London comprehensive school for two thousands boys and girls. It was an exciting, fearsome, exhilarating, dangerous, enormously rewarding and memorable period. I was gratified for simply having survived. In the first five years, the school was transformed from one to which parents refused to send their sons and daughters into one of the most heavily oversubscribed comprehensives in London.

My religious beliefs have a strong hold on my life but my relationship with the Lord is quite informal. On my appointment to a post that might well have finished me off, I prayed that, should I survive for ten years, I would like him to find me something else to do. Prayer is a dangerous activity. You need to be careful what you ask for.

The school's success was achieved by introducing discipline – a boo word for some educational theorists – so that there was order instead of disorder, and by appointing staff who shared my view that, while all young people are not equally clever, each and every one is equally *valuable.* By these two simple steps, the ethos of the school was transformed. Firstly, conditions were established that enabled teachers to focus on teaching effectively rather than practising riot control. Secondly, the needs of every boy and girl were met, regardless of academic ability, or lack of it.

The second of those features was a radical departure from previous practice. The greatest share of the school's resources had been devoted to the cleverest young people whose academic achievements might, it was believed, enhance the school's reputation. Provision for the least able didn't amount to a row of beans, so they smashed the place up. I was warned by the school keeper to keep away from the terrace below the main teaching block while the school was in session as chairs and desks were frequently pitched out of windows six storeys above. The terrace was known as Bomb Alley.

My introducing a remedial department to address the needs of those left behind in the process of teaching and learning, and paying its head the same as those in charge of the two most highly regarded subjects – English and mathematics – was regarded with incredulity by the deputy head, who had served my predecessor and who had expected to be appointed to the headship on his departure.

The ethos of the school changed dramatically. With the abolition of disorder in classrooms and corridors, the cost of repairing smashed windows and doors, and of removing graffiti from the walls, plummeted. The money saved was devoted to the appointment of a team of teachers of reading for those boys and girls entering the school at eleven who were illiterate. Eight small classrooms were built to accommodate this important work.

At prizegiving, a girl who had entered the school at 11 with a reading age of 7, and who had brought her reading age up to her chronological age in just two terms, was applauded as heartily as a young man in the sixth form who had top grades in his A levels and was going up to Oxford. The message of equal value was getting across.

One of the school governors told me I was a magician. I said that was nonsense and insisted that the school's success was down to common sense. I quoted the words of Cardinal Basil Hume when he was headmaster of Ampleforth: 'Leadership often means simply persuading people to do what they should have done in the first place.' I wondered what on earth the governing body of the school had been doing in the years when the school's reputation had been so bad, but resisted the temptation.

Having survived the joys and sorrows of head-mastering in London for ten years, I was invited to assume the leadership of an embryonic trade union called the Professional Association of Teachers (PAT). It catered for teachers who were opposed in principle to the idea of going on strike. It had been established because of growing militancy by the leaders of the big unions, who had their members bring closure to schools in pursuit of better pay. The motto of the new union, emblazoned by its franking machine on outgoing mail, was: Children First – Strike Never.

After attracting a few thousand members, the pioneers who had set up the Association looked round for someone to appoint as its first General Secretary. It surprised me to be invited to take up this post. Education politics had never been a feature of my experience. The Education Officer of the Inner London Education Authority said to me: 'Whoever takes that job is in for a fight. It's just right for you.'

Leaving London had never crossed my mind. However, it appeared to me that the Lord, who had always guided my life, was behind the invitation. Resigning my headship, I prepared to move to the Midlands, saying in my prayers: 'Here's another fine mess you're getting me into. I hope you know what you're doing.' He to whom that message was addressed did, of course, know exactly what he wanted me to do. The new union had nearly 50,000 members by the time of my retirement twelve years later and its voice was heard in all the places that mattered when it came to education.

On a bright but windy day in the summer of 1986, Her Majesty hung the OBE on my lapel and asked me to tell her about myself. I explained that I was the General Secretary of a teachers' union. 'Oh', she said, 'these are difficult times in education.' They certainly were. Schools up and down the country were closed by teachers taking strike action. It was good to know that the

Queen was aware of it. She asked me what was special about my organization and I explained that members declined to take strike action under any circumstances. My two minutes were up but she before whom I stood wanted to know more. 'I see', she said, 'so your teachers never strike?' 'No ma'am.' 'What never, ever?' 'No ma'am, never, ever.' 'Well', she reiterated, 'these are difficult times in education.' She congratulated me on my award and I bowed and moved on.

That afternoon, I was scheduled to take a delegation into the Department of Education to meet Kenneth Baker, the Secretary of State, to argue the case for improving teachers' pay and conditions of service. That carried into effect the Association's belief in the force of argument rather than the argument of force, a pithy pronouncement taken from the writings of Ralf Dharendorf, the Director of the London School of Economics, the LSE, where I was once an undergraduate.

Of the five Secretaries of State with whom I had dealt over the years, Baker was the most pleasant and ready to listen. He was also the cleverest and the most difficult to read. But, for once, I had the drop on him. He swept us in and said, 'Well, these are difficult time in education.' I replied, 'Yes, Minister, Her Majesty the Queen and I have just been saying the same thing to one another.' He was gobsmacked!

There was an ice cream van parked outside the Department of Education as our delegation emerged. The Chairman of the Association was so pleased with the meeting that had taken place that he surprised us all by buying us ice creams. Standing in the street licking a large ice cream cornet, I thought that some of those I had once taught would be astonished to see it. A memorable day had ended most memorably.

Religion

When the missionaries first came to Africa,
they had the Bible and we had the land.
They said, 'Let us pray.' We closed our eyes.
When we opened them again, we had the
Bible and they had the land.

Archbishop Desmond Tutu

A headmaster died and arrived at the Pearly
Gates to be greeted not only, as expected,
by Saint Peter, but also by the Devil. He
raised his eyebrows, as headmasters do, but
was told by Saint Peter: 'We've just gone
comprehensive'.

Vincent Rosewell

Governments of all sizes and shapes are in
danger of creating an unhealthy and even
dangerous culture in our society. If we have
a problem, the answer is more law. I do not
question the need for law; what I question is

a culture that may have the effect of letting us all off the hook of personal responsibility.

Rt Rev John Gladwin

A faith is not acquired by reason. One does not fall in love or enter the church as a result of logical persuasion. Reason may defend an act of faith, but only after the act has been committed. A faith grows like a tree. Its crown points to the sky and its roots grow downward into the past and are nourished by the dark sap of the ancestral humus.

Arthur Koestler

As you pass this little church, be sure to plan a visit, so when at last you're carried in, God won't ask, 'Who is it?'

Church Poster

AS YOU LIKE IT

Shakespeare's wife said, 'Is this as you like it?'
As she called him to dinner one day.
He replied, 'Let me first complete Hamlet,
I really must finish this play.'

'Last week', said his wife, ''twas Othello,
Who strangled his wife when in bed.
You are a fanatical fellow:
Your scribbling makes me see red.'

'Can't stop now', said her husbandly mate,
'I've got lots more ideas to set down.
Of comedies, killings and matters of state.
My plays will one day be renowned.'

'Oh, come off it', said Mrs Shakespeare,
'You'll never be famous like some
Who are authors of note that we know dear.
You'll soon be forgotten old chum.'

Shakespeare spoke of his wife in the ale house
When having a totty of rum:
'Anne hath a way of being a grouse;
There's nary a time she's much fun.

But one day my plays will be taught
To children who choose English lit.
Boys and girls of all kinds and all sorts
Will have to learn stuff I have writ.'

In a tavern nearby the Globe theatre
William chatted at length with his mates.
'What's next?' said Fat John, a big eater,
Whose appetite was escalate.

'I'm thinking', said the great playwright,
'Of inventing a chap just like you,
Whose protruberant belly's a wonderous sight
For he boozes so much it ain't true.

Falstaff will not be real gentry,
He'll be a great lumbering fool
And people will cheer at his entry
As he causes disorder to rule.'

'What I'd like', said a young bearded player
Who performed on the stage with the rest,
'Is a part as a villainous slayer
With murderous plans for his guests.

As You Like It

How about a monsterous Scot,
Egged on by three wickedy witches?
The Scots are a murderous lot:
Such a play should bring us great riches.

And the wife should be evil as well
She'd come on dripping blood and all gory,
Then go mad and be heading for hell:
That will make a right lively story.'

'What I'd like', said one chap, full of bounce,
'Is to have a big battle on stage.'
Shakespeare said, 'We would have to announce
That folk must *imagine* war's rage.'

The Agincourt battle took place
With trumpets and all sorts of din.
Henry Five made a really great speech
That Sir Laurence made famous on film.

So what's there to ask, in the end,
Of the plays that Will Shakespeare has writ?
That, when you choose to attend,
As you leave you will say you liked it.

Rules for Teachers

Rules from long ago displayed in the Tauranga District Museum in New Zealand:

You will not marry during the term of your contract.

You are not to keep company with men.

You must be home between the hours of 8 pm and 6 am unless attending a school function.

You may not loiter in ice cream stores.

You may not travel beyond the city limits without the permission of the Chairman of the Board.

You may not ride in a carriage with a man unless he is your father or your brother.

You may not smoke cigarettes.

You may not dress in bright colours.

You may under no circumstance dye your hair.

You must wear at least two petticoats.

Your dresses must not be any shorter than two inches above the ankle.

To keep the school room clean and ready you must:

1 *Sweep the floor at least once daily.*
2 *Scrub the floor with hot, soapy water at least once a week.*
3 *Clean the blackboard at least once a day.*
4 *Start the fire at 7 am.*

Source: Sevenoaks Teachers' Centre

SPONGIFORM SCHOOLING

In Britain in 1986, bovine spongiform encepha-lopathy (BSE) was discovered to be infecting cattle. A fatal disease affecting the brain and spinal cord, it became known as mad cow disease. Three million cattle were slaughtered in the ensuing five years. My education column in the Daily Telegraph was at this time devoted on one occasion to BSE in schools, which has yet to be completely eradicated.

The recent discovery that nearly one million young people in England and Wales cannot read properly is not difficult to explain. They are suffering from bland spongiform education (BSE).

The sickness is due to the victims having been given an easy time of it at school. They should have been taught to recognize the letters of the alphabet, get the hang of spelling and look inside books. Instead, teachers with no commitment to academic rigour, and little command of the written word themselves, have allowed young people to spend their time exploring the boundaries of the social interface. As a result, the nation's children have gone soft in the head.

As a practising headmaster, I once told a lecture theatre full of student teachers that the first thing they had to do on teaching practice was teach the children to sit still, shut up and listen. Their tutor told me afterwards, 'You are an educational coelacanth.' Seeing how that species of fish has survived the changes and chances of this fleeting world for millions of years, the label gave me some comfort.

At this time of the school year, 16 year-olds up and down the country are sitting their first public examinations. The GCSE season is upon us. The inadequacy of many of the candidates is due to their never having been made to pay attention to their teachers, which is necessary for learning to take place. Discovering how to handle the riches of English literature can be a difficult and tedious process at the start. It just cannot be done in the atmosphere prevailing in some schools, where the very notion of requiring young people to do something they do not immediately enjoy gives the shakes to the classroom *avant garde.*

School BSE, or mad classroom disease, exists largely as a result of the ridiculous notion that a teacher's primary duty is to make lessons interesting. That is a heresy in precisely the sense that the great Erasmus used the word. He insisted that to be heretical was not necessarily to utter a false doctrine but to elevate part of the truth as if it were the whole.

Part of the truth about teaching is that young people learn better if they are interested. But the whole truth is that not everything can be made interesting at every stage of the educational process. What is more, some pupils are quite determined never to be interested in lessons, for reasons that have nothing to do with the curriculum, teaching methods or anything else it is in the power of teachers to determine.

If the Secretary of State for Education wants to raise standards of literacy in this country at a stroke, I will tell him what to do. He should introduce a short Bill laying down a statutory requirement that every child should have a spelling test every Friday afternoon. Mind you, if my advice were taken by those who govern the country, it would be essential for every teacher to be supplied with a dictionary. A good many have spelling difficulties themselves. That is part of the problem.

It is not much good our complaining about young people being illiterate and ignoring the world of books: they are as they are because of the state of the adult population. If there were a survey of mature adults like the one just carried out with 16 to 20 year-olds, the percentage of those who never open a book would not be very different. In many homes today, there is no room for a bookcase, what with all the television, video and music-playing equipment for which room has to be found. Technology that assaults the senses has taken over from literature that feeds the mind.

If more than a million young people in this country do not have the habit of reading books, it is because they come from bookless homes where their parents live bookless lives, and because they attend schools where a proper grasp of the English language is not given sufficient priority. Something needs to be done urgently before we are faced with a whole generation with spongiform brains.

School to University

Girls wouldn't be able to concentrate on their work in a mixed school with boys around. They have admitted it to me.

Girls' Grammar School Headmistress

How would you prove that the British Isles occupy the best geographical position in the world?

Examination question set
by the Bradford School Board 1901

In our school, Mrs Richards looks after us all the time. She is not always good-tempered though. Sometimes she is not good-tempered when it is something else that has upset her that is not what we have done. But we understand and do not mind too much because she is nice really. She is kind to us, I think, and we all think, because she is kind inside. When I grow up I want to be like Mrs Richards.

Sally (9)

*Briefly, we put living before learning. At 90
I'm too damned tired to write any more
about Summerhill. We have a waiting list a
yard long, mostly furriners.*

Letter from A S Neill of Summerhill

*Once someone enters a university as an
undergraduate, the minimum of compulsion
is best. We don't make them do anything; we
just fail them if they don't. They have to bear
the consequences of their own decisions. It's
called growing up.*

Michael Creech,
Fielden Professor of French at UCL

PAUL ROBESON
PLAYS OTHELLO

The cast: Othello   Paul Robeson
           Desdemona Mary Ure
           Iago   Sam Wannamaker
           Cassio   Albert Finney

In seven decades of theatergoing, one moment still lives with me like no other. The year was 1959, the place the Shakespeare Memorial Theatre at Stratford-upon-Avon. It was spring, when new life and hope stirs the emotions.

At last granted a visa to leave the United states after repeated refusals during the McCarthy era, Paul Robeson came to play Othello. Famous as a magnificent baritone singer, he was the first black man to be invited to play a part for which famous Shakespearean actors like Olivier had been blacked up.

Robeson's performance was perceived as a turning point not only in theatrical history but also in the battle for world-wide racial harmony. In the words of one critic, Robeson brought a new life and a new dimension to one of Shakespeare's greatest plays. The arts page of one national newspaper said: 'The moment Paul Robeson strode on to the stage, his massive figure dwarfing everyone around him, the audience was spellbound.'

The following commemorates the occasion:

> Hugely black, with voice that boomed
> As if from some cavernous tomb,
> Othello, from his great height,
> Towered over his fair wife.
> Golden-haired was Desdemona,
> And fitly meek in her persona.
> Had this union of black and white
> Been waiting till the time was right?
> At last, full harmony of races
> Sought then, and still, in many places.
> But, led to doubt his wife by Iago,
> Whose villainy knew no embargo,
> The serpent who was for Adam too wise
> Had come again in different guise.
> So, man's best hopes are undermined
> By evil lying close at hand.
> Performances are of their time,
> Showing what's in people's minds,
> What they believe and they dismiss,
> What they accept and they resist.
> When this Othello strode the stage

Paul Robeson Plays Othello

Wannamaker was his plague,
Whispering wickedness in his ears
And generating mighty fears.
Just as McCarthy had held forth,
Corrupting many people's thoughts,
Evil and hatred Iago brought
To the mind of his great master
And so led him into disaster.
Othello loved not wisely but too well,
Falling under Iago's spell,
Who trapped good Cassio in his plans,
Made him a part of his dark schemes.
By such theatricality
People are shaken from their lethargy.
To each new age the playwright brings
Words in season with new meanings.
Othello's message still endures
And calls to us, that we ensure
We're not too ready to be trusting
Lest we do cause our own destruction.

History

*A people who no longer remembers has lost
its history and therefore its soul.*

Alexander Solzhenitsyn

War is the engine of history.

Leon Trotsky

*The human story does not always unfold like
a mathematical calculation on the principle
that two and two make four. Sometimes
in life they make five or minus three; and
sometimes the blackboard topples down in
the middle of the sum and leaves the class in
disorder and the pedagogue with a black eye.*

Winston Churchill

Theodore White, the American historian and political journalist, likens leading any organization to being at the head of one of the great convoys of wagons, known as prairie schooners, heading West in the days of the American pioneers:

The country ahead is full of unknown dangers and fresh promise. In the procession there are those who trudge on foot, those who ride in the wagons, those who go by horse. On and on they go, some infuriated by the slowness of the pace and others who insist the journey pause because the pace is too fast. Up there at the head of the advance column, the leaders quarrel bitterly among themselves. They disagree as to what course to take, at what pace, at what cost. They know that much later they will be judged by some archaeologist's description of their route, of their perception, of their decision. But they know that now, right now, they can hold on to their leadership not by largeness of vision or logic of plan but only by the approval of those who follow.

SERVING EUROPE

Serving for four years at the end of the 1980s as a UK delegate to the economic and social assembly of the European Union, my purpose in this memoir is to lighten the debate about our country's membership, and to make some serious points by the way.

The assembly had nearly two hundred members in my time, appointed by member states to advise the Council of Ministers on economic and social issues. It is a gathering of experts responsible for ensuring that, when the Council is of a mind to deal with a matter of economic and social importance, it knows what it is doing.

The notion that experts from vastly different member states will be able to come to one mind on any matter is scarcely credible. Debates often resulted in the production of documents so full of compromises that their usefulness was questionable.

But no matter. The assembly provided an opportunity for men and women with political ambitions at home, or who had dropped out of the political running there, to practice politics in exchange for generous financial benefits.

My seat in the assembly was next to a morbidly obese French delegate for whom meal breaks were no less important than assembly business. In the middle of a debate about banking, he nudged me and said: 'Pierre, is time to eat. I will propose we adjourn. You will support me, yes?' I declined, insisting that the banking debate was critical and we should complete it first. The Frenchman simply shrugged and left the chamber. When he came back two hours later, well fed and slightly sozzled, I thought he would want to know the outcome of the debate he had missed. He said: 'No, no. We will wait to see what the Council decides. If we don't like it, we won't do it anyway.' I soon learned that the readiness of the UK to honour any decisions taken in Brussels was regarded with amusement by some. The Brits were regarded as a pretty uptight lot who took proceedings rather too seriously.

Queueing one day to book in at the airport on my homeward journey, I found myself behind the worst type of Englishman abroad. He was giving the Belgian booking clerk a thoroughly unpleasant time over his seating on board. Stepping up to book in, I felt obliged to apologize for the behaviour of my countryman. The clerk smiled knowingly and said: 'Thank you, sir. As a matter of fact, you are both taking the same flight home. But his luggage is going to Hong Kong.' Over my four years serving in Brussels, I learned not to upset Belgian officials of any kind.

I also learned that some delegates in the assembly paid little attention to what was going on. On one occasion it was announced that there were no interpreters available to occupy the Greek desk in the cabins around the assembly chamber. However, we were told, the Greek delegation was happy for business to proceed. They did not wish to prevent debate going ahead, although some would not be able to understand what was going on. One Greek member switched on his microphone and said, 'We never do anyway', and laughed. An Italian sitting behind me loudly whispered to those around him, 'He's not joking.'

The English sense of humour does not readily translate into other EU languages. Douglas Hogg, son of Lord Hailsham, who once said that anyone who voted Labour had to be stark raving bonkers, came to address the assembly. An English delegate had been appointed to give a vote of thanks. He declared that Mr Hogg had spoken well and that, to steal a phrase from his illustrious father, anyone who didn't realize it must be stark raving bonkers. The speaker paused, expecting laughter. The interpreters in their cabins round the chamber were shrugging at one another, unable to understand the joke and translate it.

The building on the Rue Ravenstein that

accommodates the economic and social assembly of the EU looks out across a beautiful part of Brussels. The Grand Place is only a short walk away, with its magnificent architecture, erected by the mediaeval guilds long ago. It was a privilege to have a reason to spend time there. But there remains with me a feeling of guilt. The cost of assembly meetings, in time and money, sometimes seemed hard to justify for our collective wisdom was as often as not ignored.

Around the walls of the assembly there were several prominent no smoking notices, put there after a clear decision to have a smoke-free environment. But members of the Italian delegation ignored the notices and lit up when they felt like it. That's a sort of EU parable. Those who serve it only bother to conform to its decisions if it suits them, otherwise they brush them aside like a horse swishing its tail to get rid of flies.

So, here's a question to think about. Is it reasonable to expect a conglomeration of countries such as the European Union to work together and make collective decisions that will be honoured and respected by all? My experience leads me to quote the immortal words of that great philosopher of the tennis court, John MacEnroe, when an umpire's decision went against him: 'You cannot be serious!'

Advice from the Famous

When in doubt, stick your left out.

> Henry Cooper

The only place success comes before work is in the dictionary.

> Vidal Sassoon

If you can keep your head while all about you are losing theirs, you don't understand what's going on.

> Tom Roseingrave,
> Irish delegate to the EU

We only learn by living through it all ourselves, not from the experience of others.

> Alexander Solzhenitsyn

*I read in a book that a man called
Christ went about doing good. It is very
disconcerting that I am so easily satisfied
with just going about.*

Kagawa of Japan

*Anybody who enjoys being in the House of
Commons probably needs psychiatric help.*

Ken Livingstone

GENERATION
BORN TO LOSE

On 8 August 1991, my regular education column in the Daily Telegraph *was devoted to problems presented in schools by the emergence of the one-parent family. A speech I had made about that had caused uproar in the media. Five national newspapers reported my comments on their front pages; several editorials and feature articles analysed my speech; there were interviews on radio and television. Much of the coverage was hostile. My subsequent piece for the* Daily Telegraph *appears below, headlined by the newspaper as at the top of this page (not my title).*

In my valedictory conference speech after nearly twelve years as leader of the Professional Association of Teachers, I raised the issue last week of the relationship between family life and educational performance. If you have not observed the reaction to that, you must have been living on the planet Mars in the last few days.

The connection between children's family circumstances and their performance in school is an emotional minefield. It passes judgment on every living adult who has attempted to raise children. Has the success or failure of your offspring been down to you? You bet your life it has. Almost everything a child achieves in school, or fails to achieve, may be traced back to what happens at home.

That being so, there is disturbing news for our society. By the end of this decade, most children will be brought up in one-parent families. That prediction comes from Gingerbread, the one-parent family support group.

What are likely to be the consequences of a new social structure, with the young being raised by just one parent rather than two? We already know something of the answer, and it is not a happy one. Professor Albert Halsey of Nuffield College, Oxford, a distinguished sociologist, recently said that he shuddered for the next generation of children, brought up in one-parent families. They would do less well at school, be more likely to end up unemployed, be more inclined to get into trouble with the law.

Teachers are well placed to add to the list of deprivations. Children with only one parent often play truant, show signs of insecurity in their relationships with others, need more care and attention from their teachers than others.

Yes, there are many children who are brought up very successfully, despite having only one parent to care for them. But such successes are exceptions that prove the rule that children need two parents to grow and flourish as best they may.

Most single parents are not in that state as a result of war or natural disaster. That is the heart of the problem facing our society. We have the highest divorce rate in the European Community and the greatest number of one-parent families, both as a result of choices people have made.

Here is a girl who chooses to have a child without even considering marriage. Here is a man who fathers a child, then removes himself when the responsibility for raising it interferes with his liberal lifestyle. As a Methodist Minister I spend a good deal of time trying to give help and support to the casualties of these arrangements.

A few months ago, I was in a television studio full of teenage mothers whose boy friends had left them more or less destitute. When I said that men should abstain from sexual activity if they were not prepared to fulfil their obligations upon conceiving children, the girls all cheered. But they made it clear to me afterwards that they themselves were not ready to abstain.

Anyone who raises the issue of the devastating effect of the emergence of the one-parent family is bound to be criticized. First, doing such a thing is taken as an attack on young women struggling to raise children on their own. What could be more cruel? Second, we have a one-parent industry in this country, whose intention is to justify the new social structure, and thereby provide a basis for insisting that the state fund it. There is much gold to be had from government if ordinary citizens can be persuaded to pay up and shut up about the one-parent family. But silence on this issue will ensure that, a decade or two from now, children with two parents will be in a minority. Is that what we want?

Courtship and After

Courtship is that period during which a girl
decides whether or not she can do any better.

Billy Graham

I would like to thank my wife for her help
in winning this award. Without her steady
doubt and ridicule I would not have had the
determination to go on.

Michael Aspel, Receiving a
Variety Club of Great Britain Award

A good wife is far more precious than jewels.
The heart of her husband trusts in her. She
rises while it is yet night and provides food
for her household. She seeks wool and flax
and all her household are well clothed.
She opens her mouth with wisdom and the
teaching of kindness is on her tongue.

Holy Bible, Revised Standard
Version, Proverbs 31

When a report appeared about a woman flying a supersonic fighter in the RAF, stating that she was still able to chat while flying faster than the speed of sound, the following appeared in the letters columns of the newspaper that had printed the story:

To many a husband, your report will come as no surprise. My wife is able to chat in a wide variety of extreme conditions. I feel sure that, not only would she be able to do so while breaking the sound barrier, but she would also be able to complete her shopping list.

Robert C Swindlehurst
to the *Daily Telegraph*

The way you live your life, it's a good job there are two of us to live it.

Shirley Margaret Dawson

ON BEING DISABLED

When the Disability Discrimination Act was passed, Mr Justice Morison, the President of the Employment Appeal Tribunal in London, arranged a seminar for the judges and lay members of the Tribunal in preparation for cases likely to be brought before them. With great acuity, the President invited as keynote speaker Herbert Massie, a leading figure in the promotion of employment rights for the disabled who, a year after the seminar, became Chairman of the new Disability Rights Commission. A man whose contorted body was in a wheelchair with more special features than a top-of-the-range Mercedes, Massie put on an unforgettable performance. My notes from that event provide the basis of what follows.

'Who is disabled?' asked the speaker. No response. So he said: 'If you are wearing glasses, take them off and stamp on them.' Still no response. Then this: 'If you can't live without your glasses, you're disabled, like me. I can't live without my wheelchair. The only difference between us is the nature and extent of our disabilities.'

Massie warned us that we were destined to deal with all sorts of disabilities in the years ahead, some of which we will not have come across before. 'We all', he asserted, 'either die young or get disabled.' He prophesied that far more disabled people than in the past would in future expect to be employed. Disability would no longer debar people from going to work. He referred to the – obviously fictitious – story of an aide to Horatio Nelson who didn't like the idea of men being admitted to the navy who were not fully up to scratch physically. 'We can't have disabled sailors', he told the Admiral. Nelson's reply is not recorded.

Asked what a seriously disabled person needed to be happy in employment, Massie said a sense of humour. His own was very evident. 'Of course', he said, 'I sometimes get a bit depressed by the shape of my body. To cheer myself up, I drive down to the coast in the summer and look at all the people on the beach in their bathing costumes and realize I'm not so bad.'

He told the gathering of judges and captains of industry and trade union leaders who sit in judgment at the Employment Appeal Tribunal that it's often not a disabled person who has a big problem but the people around him or her. 'That applies now in the work place and will become more critical in dealing with discrimination now that it is illegal. The new regulations require employers to make reasonable adjustments in order to accommodate a disabled person.' Fixing us firmly with his eye, and amusing himself at our expense, he said: 'Much time and money is going to be spent as employment lawyers argue the toss before you over what is and what is not a reasonable adjustment'. And, dear reader, so it has proved.

The Church

Church is like a swimming pool. All the noise is at the shallow end.

Andrew Marr, BBC Radio 4 Start the Week

Verse on a tombstone at Colne Parish Church:

When thou reads the state of me,
Think of the glass that runs for thee.

One may sometimes attend church for a year and hear excellent discourses on international peace, industrial justice, civil liberties, sex relations, social ethics in every phase, but rarely or never a word to help one's poor little soul in its effort to enter into communion with the Eternal.

Vida Scudder

Words of John Bunyan to be seen in the chapel at the University of Aberystwyth:

Here one may, without much molestation, be thinking about where he is, whence he came, what he has done and to what the King has called him

It's just called The Bible now. We dropped the word Holy to give it a more mass market appeal

Judith Young,
Hodder & Stoughton Publishers

When I go to hear a preacher in his pulpit, I like him to appear to be fighting bees.

Abraham Lincoln

WORD GAMES

'It means making happy and unexpected discoveries by accident', said Josh Stevens, a teacher of English at the local grammar school, to his friend Simon Evans, an insurance agent. 'You mean like stuff I plant in my garden actually coming up. My wife calls me the Dark Destroyer and prefers it if I leave the gardening to her. She's brilliant. I'm hopeless. I've planted some cabbages in our vegetable patch this year but they won't come to anything.'

'What are you two on about?' said Harry Brewer, a car salesman whose only interest was the likely performance of Crystal Palace against Arsenal. The three men were in the saloon bar of the Oak & Apple in Selhurst at Saturday lunch time, on the way to the match. They had all been at school together many years before. Although their careers had taken widely different directions, they still lived in Selhurst and still met to support the Eagles. They could recall the days when, as small boys, they were lifted over the heads of the football crowd and deposited at the fence beside the pitch.

Harry repeated his question: 'What are you two

on about?' 'I was explaining what serendipity is', responded Josh. 'Get away', said Harry, 'there's no such word. It sounds like one Ken Dodd made up.' 'If you aren't careful', responded Josh, 'you will be discumnockerated.' 'And end up titifelarious', said Simon.

'Doddy's at the Fairfield Hall in Croydon at Christmas', said Harry. 'The stage hands won't be pleased. Last year, they couldn't get him off the stage on Christmas Eve. Once he's got an audience going, he'll keep performing. Better than going back to a lonely hotel room'.

'Did you know', said Simon, 'that he started out as the Kleeneze man in Knotty Ash? It's an actual place outside Liverpool. Doddy was a door-to-door salesman with a case full of domestic cleaning materials. That's where he got his tickling stick from. Knotty Ash folk say he was a right comedian on the doorstep. So, he took to the stage and probably surprised himself, discovering that he was more than a doorstep joker.' 'And that', asserted Simon, 'is serendipity', showing off the latest addition to his vocabulary. 'Would you like to know where the word comes from?' asked Josh. 'Give over', said Harry. 'Tell us after the match. How are we going to beat the Gunners? We could get clobbered this afternoon.'

Leaving the pub, the three men made the way on foot to the Crystal Palace ground at Selhurst Park, talking about the forthcoming match. Once inside the ground, they headed for the terraces preferring, as Harry put it when asked, to be among the real supporters rather than among the money men in the stand. As they settled themselves against one of the metal stanchions lining the terrace, Josh opined that the day would come when fixed seating would be mandatory in major football stadia. 'Just watch what happens to ticket prices then', said Simon prophetically.

As the sound of 'Glad All Over', the Eagles' anthem, rang round the ground, the team trotted on to the pitch, followed by the Arsenal eleven, whose main striker, a tall, muscular and shining black Ivorian named Sam Aboga, had been the star of the Ivory Coast team that won the Africa Cup. He had scored in every Arsenal match since the English football season had started two months before. 'Our defence will never hold him', said Josh.

Thirteen minutes into the game, Aboga hurtled up the field, leaving behind him a trail of unsuccessful attempts to tackle him. Entering the home team's penalty area, he prepared to shoot with only the Crystal Palace goalkeeper, Jack Wallace, to beat. Wallace hurled himself at the striker and, throwing his arms round the striker's legs to prevent a certain goal, brought him down. The Arsenal supporters went berserk and the Gunners' team screamed at the referee, who raised a red card over Jack Wallace, who trudged from the field. 'Now we've had it', said Simon Evans to his two companions on the terrace, 'We can't take off another player and send on our reserve goalie. We haven't got one.'

There was a lengthy break in play while Crystal Palace sorted that out. None of the Eagles' players on the pitch wanted to take the goalkeeper's jumper and gloves. In the end, a young lad named Phil Choker, who had only just been promoted from the youth team, got the job. Of average height and sturdily built, he played in the mid-field in the youth team, operating as an old-fashioned centre-half. He was seen as a future playmaker, with a keen football brain. But he had never played in goal and took his place between the posts in high dudgeon. 'Why me?', he muttered to himself, 'Why me?'

'Aboga will murder him', said Harry, 'we'll be lucky to get away with a six-nil thrashing. Choker is the right name for him.' From the Arsenal supporters came the cry, 'Attack! Attack! Attack!' As their forwards responded, the defenders in front of them stood their ground with the help of the Eagles' forwards, with the manager signalling to the whole team to join the defence. 'Come on the nine men', chanted the supporters of the home team, having nothing better to make a noise about. 'There are ten of us', Phil Choker ruefully told himself, 'but I suppose I don't count.'

Aboga gathered the ball twenty yards out and

shot it like a rocket towards the top left corner of the goal. It was one of his favourite ploys and he smiled to himself as it sailed safe and true towards its target. 'Nobody's going to stop that!' cried the Arsenal manager from the touchline. But as the ball sailed over the heads of the opposition, curving into the goal, Phil Choker hurled himself into the air and, stretching out one hand to intercept the ball, pushed it over the bar. 'Great save', said Bill Bower, the Crystal Palace captain, patting the newcomer to goalkeeping on the head, 'that was terrific.' 'I didn't know I could do that', came the response. Jock Angus, a highland Scott, who had come on a free transfer from Inverness Caledonian Thistle, put his arm round the goalkeeper and said, 'Well, laddie, ye ken the noo, ye ken the noo.'

Phil Choker continued to amaze, making a further three spectacular saves before half-time. The Crystal Palace chanting army, as they were known, had devised a new cry and gave vent to it as the players left the field: 'Chokey, Chokey, he's the greatest goalie', rang out. 'He'll never keep them out in the second half', said Simon.

The story of the second half delighted the home fans but did no good for the image of professional football. As the mighty Arsenal team became more and more frustrated by the increasingly effective Palace defence, which became more and more confident as they had a brilliant goalkeeper behind them. Tempers frayed. Aboga, who had a reputation for violent play, bounded about in the penalty area as Arsenal took a corner. As Phil Choker rose to punch the ball away, Aboga surreptitiously punched him in the back. But the foul had not been surreptitious enough. The referee waved a red card at him.

Denied the services of their main striker, Arsenal's attack became increasingly disorganized, but it remained difficult for the Eagles to get out of their half of the field. Their defence remained resolute and their goalkeeper continued to make spectacular saves. After one such, he hurled the ball out to a the wing where Jock Angus controlled it, then raced towards the Arsenal goal, which was devoid of defenders. As Jock thumped the ball into the net, the stadium erupted. Three minutes later, the referee blew his whistle to bring to an end an unlikely Palace victory. Spectators ran on to the pitch and attempted to parade Jock Angus shoulder high round the stadium. He pushed them away, shouting, 'Not me, ye daft sassenachs. Chokey. He won the game for us.'

As the young man named was lifted and carried off, the BBC Radio commentator was telling the world he had made no fewer than eight great saves. Interviewed afterwards, Phil Choker was asked if he thought his future lay with goalkeeping. 'I suppose so', he said, 'I enjoyed myself, but I didn't know I was any good at it until today.'

'A clear case of serendipity,' said Josh Stevens over a pint at the Oak and Apple to his two friends on the way home. 'I can see that', said Simon, 'but I still think it's a funny sort of word.' 'Well', responded Josh, 'its origin is a bit peculiar. Serendip is the original name of Ceylon and there was a sort of fairy tale called *The Three Princes of Serendip* who were always making discoveries by accident. Serendipity means just that. You could say that Phil Choker discovered he was a brilliant goalkeeper by accident.' 'And a good job he did', said Simon.

When he got home Josh discovered that, while he had been away, the power had gone off while his wife had been ironing. 'I found the fuse box and fixed it', she said. 'I have always told you to leave the electrics in this house alone', said Josh, 'electricity is dangerous. You should have left it for me to deal with.' 'Oh, piffle', came the reply, 'It wasn't difficult. I never realized how easy it was. What's that long word you use for that sort of thing?'

Getting On

*One Saturday we decided with two friends
that we would like to go to the midnight
movie at the local cinema. I rang to book
the seats and mentioned that we were all
OAPs. 'Madam', was the reply, 'there are no
reductions at this time of night – you should
all be in bed.'*

Anne Philips, 'Not Dead Yet'
column in *The Times*

*The days of the maestro are over.
Nevertheless, under that new, self-effacing,
I-am-just-one-of-the-boys, merely-a-tool-of-
the-gods exterior, lies a heart of pure vanity.*

Andre Previn, BBC 1 Omnibus
'Who Needs a Conductor?'

*Say not thou, what is the cause that former
days were better than these, for thou dost not
enquire wisely concerning this.*

Holy Bible Ecclesiastes 7

First there was putting hot-water bottles to it,
Then there was seeing what an osteopath
  could do,
Then trying drugs to coax the thing and woo
  it,
Then came the time when he knew that he
  was through.

John Betjeman's 'Inevitable'

Unless there is some specific physical or
mental illness, the elderly need not become
slow-witted, stiff in mind and body, and
generally ill. In the Far East, you see elderly
people sitting cross-legged on the ground. Yet
all they did to achieve this suppleness was
never stop sitting on the ground.

Moyna Bremner on Western Society

Soon after my grandmother's death we were
amused to find among the odds and ends in
her dressing table drawer a bottle labelled
Might Be Aspirin.

Jean Gibbs to *The Times*

HUMAN SEXUALITY

For several years back in the 1970s, I was a speaker at an annual conference on family planning at University College Hospital Medical School in London. It was a multi-disciplinary event attended by professionals in medicine, nursing, teaching, social and welfare work, the law, policing, and associated activities. My task was to deal with sex education in schools. What follows is a summary of my contributions.

Let me begin by putting the issue of sex in its proper context. A great many problems young people have, and those not so young, in this area of human behaviour arise because struggling with sexuality is just part of a general malaise.

What do we expect to be going on when we talk about sex education? Are we simply trying to give young people a check list of ways to avoid disaster? You would think so if you listen to some so-called experts. But sexuality cannot be isolated from a person's total humanity. Youngsters who get into trouble over sex are usually in trouble over a whole load of other things as well.

Mrs Blake arrived at my study one morning with her fourteen-year-old daughter Janice in tow. 'Oh Mr Dawson' she said, clearly exasperated, 'Janice has gone and done what her sister done in the fourth year. She let that toe rag Jimmy West break her in behind the Odeon and now she's got a bump. Mr Dawson, she knows how to not get pregnant. I've told her and told her. I don't want her to miss her exams like her sister.'

Janice, a bright but sullen girl who had been in trouble in and out of school many times, came out with the South London mantra we were used to hearing from those who rarely counted the cost of their misbehaviour: 'I ain't bovvered.'

Janice was not pregnant because she was ignorant. She was pregnant because in this, as in other parts of her life, she just didn't care what happened. Sex education in the sense in which it is often discussed would have done nothing for her.

One of the reasons politicians and others argue for more or better sex education is to deal with the high rate of illegitimate births among adolescent girls. 'We used to think', said one politician to me, 'that ignorance reduced promiscuity. But it doesn't seem to work that way'.

Of course it doesn't in a society where letting young people explore the boundaries of the social framework in an increasingly liberal context is the name of the game. Knowledge may actually increase promiscuity unless what is taught about sex is part of a programme of personal responsibility in all areas of life. 'You have to see if your equipment works', said a boy in a school where sex education was purely mechanistic. And after that?

'Young people must be allowed to find their own moral pathway', said one agent of the sex education industry, 'we cannot impose our values on them.' But, of course, those who talk that way are highly committed to their own view of human sexuality. They use every means at their disposal to persuade young people to share it. There are no neutrals in the battle to invade the minds of the next generation.

The message I have been preaching, since one beautiful sunny April morning in 1975 in the obstetrics wing of UCH, has been that I don't believe in sex education. It's therefore with a certain feeling of triumph that I stand before you today with my name on your programme under a different heading from sex education, namely Human Relationship Problems in Schools.

One more thing, perhaps the most important of all. What happens when a school sets out to deal properly and comprehensively with human relationships depends upon having the right teachers. A teacher does not just teach a subject – he or she teaches attitudes and values. We who presume to stand in front of a class teach what we are.

The great constitutional historian Walter Bagehot wrote more than a century ago: 'A schoolmaster should have an attitude of awe, and walk wonderingly, as if amazed at being himself.' We all remember our best teachers. Only the best are let loose in my Department of Human Relations.

In appointing teachers to develop its work, great care has had to be taken to ensure that applicants don't have a personal agenda. A woman whose face suggested that she had some tough experiences told me how pleased she was to find a school that really wanted to address the problems in the field of human relations that young people had to face. Good. But she rather spoiled her case by adding: 'I want to warn these girls against marriage.'

Whatever we do, young people *will* find their own moral pathways by which to live their lives. But they need proper guidance to find their way.

My school was opened by Lord Hunt, the leader of the team that conquered Everest. Edmund Hilary would not have reached the summit of that mighty mountain without Sherpa Tensing to guide him. Guiding boys and girls to take a responsible attitude to their behaviour, including their sexual conduct, is an enormous task because it will determine the future shape of society. There is no greater duty laid upon the teaching profession, and the other agencies represented at this conference.

Leadership

Leadership means seeing that the strong have something to strive for while the weak are not overwhelmed. There is therefore no question of treating people equally.

Basil Hume

Oswald Mosley could thrill a multitude by declaiming the explanatory notes on an income tax form.

Leeds Mercury

If St George were alive today, he would be armed not with a lance but with several flexible formulas. He would propose a conference with the dragon. He would lend the dragon a lot of money. The maiden's release would be referred to Geneva or New York, the dragon reserving all rights meanwhile.

Winston Churchill

When Gladstone was Prime Minister, he was able to spend about five months of the year at his country home in North Wales, planting the garden and felling the oak trees with respectful working men. Today, if a prime minister takes time off to spend a weekend on the water on his yacht, there is an outcry, as if the quality of his statesmanship were a direct result of the quantity of his output.

Lord Hailsham,
The Richard Dimbleby Lecture 1976

Neville Chamberlain is reputed to have admitted that he had no more control over the economy than he had over the weather. Politicians and civil servants are now near unanimous agreement that they have no more control over the weather than they have over the economy. How's that for progress!

T G F Atherton,
Arragon House, Isle of Man

THE CLASSROOM
IS A STAGE

The classroom is a stage
On which a teacher will perform with special gestures
And modes of speech theatrical.
Each in his time, or hers, plays many parts.
At first, probationer, fearful alike
Of teachers and taught; fearful most of Head,
On whose opinion swift preferment waits.
Next, proud possessor of allowances,
Growing to mark responsibilities
That make the unpromoted envious,
Convinced that idle justice sleeps unknowing.
Now in classroom full of fine confidence,
Sudden and quick in clever repartee,
Fearless in face of devious juvenile,
Seeking the bubble reputation
Even in the cannon's mouth. Then as Head,
Snatched from the classroom to be the one who says,
'It shall be thus and thus'; full of wise saws,
But now no longer loved nor understood.
Next comes translation to inspectorate,

Peter Dawson

Speaking with voice made surer than before
By distance from the fray. Last scene of all,
That ends this strange eventful history,
Is sweet retirement, with tales of children
Good or bad, or in between, remember'd well,
And Friday afternoon deliverance.
So comes surrender to oblivion,
Sans chalk, sans books to mark, sans everything.

Anon

Coming to a Conclusion

We do not see the world as it is; we see it as we are. The way we see a problem IS the problem.

Dr Bill Webster

No pleasure is worth giving up for the sake of two more years in a geriatric home in Weston-super-Mare.

Kingsley Amis

Having missed short putts because of the uproar of butterflies in an adjacent meadow, I sit under a chestnut tree beside the ninth green, enjoying that perfect peace, that peace passing all understanding, that comes at last to the man who has given up golf.

Henry Longhurst

You either die young or become disabled.

Bert Massie, Chairman of
the Disability Rights Commission

*Lester Piggott was asked if he had changed
his riding technique at any time during his
life as a jockey. He replied: 'No. It's always
the same. You have one leg each side of the
horse.'*

ISSUES IN EDUCATION

For a couple of months in 1979, The Times *and its supplements were not published because of a dispute at that most illustrious of newspapers. An adventurous entrepreneur set out to fill the gap left by the educational supplement by publishing a newspaper entitled* The Weekly Educational Review. *He approached me to write a weekly column. He said, 'You have a reputation for finding it easy to be provocative. That's want we want.' Here are three of the pieces published. The issues with which they dealt remain unresolved.*

ONE
GOODBYE TO TROUBLEMAKERS

Henry Cooper tells the story of a boxer who used to wear a ginger wig for his contests. He kept it on right up to the moment the bell went for the first round, then he would whip it off and turn to face his adversary totally bald. 'Terrified them, it did,' says Henry, 'I reckon that's how he won most of his fights.'

My grandfather was a poacher. He used to poach pheasants in the days when the gentry of what is now London suburbia kept gamekeepers. But grandad was not one to take risks. He would lay a trail of corn out of the woods into the open fields, beyond the gamekeeper's domain. Any pheasant foolish enough to follow sooner or later ended up in the old man's bag.

Fisticuffs and pheasantry are not the only activities in which an unorthodox approach pays off. Education is another, especially in the area of what might be called how-to-get-rid-of-the-undesirables. Let me start on that with an assertion. There are some children who would be better off out of the education system altogether. I do not mean they should be in special schools. I do not mean they should be in sanctuary units, dungeons for the disruptive or vaults for the villainous. I mean they should be allowed *out*; permitted to *leave*; given the right to *go*.

As Robert Bolt put it in the mouth of Sir Thomas More to say in *A Man for All Seasons,* 'I trust I make myself obscure.' An education policy for all seasons would include a degree of flexibility regarding school leavers that does not exist at the moment.

What on earth is the good of going on pretending that some of our fifteen to sixteen year olds are going to get anything further from the education system? The steady increase in special units for disruptive pupils in the last few years has solved nothing very much. The reason? Too many of the places have been taken up by senior pupils who are already beyond redemption.

One of the greatest paradoxes in education at the present time is the disproportionate amount of time and money devoted to those who reject it. Most head teachers spend half their energy dealing with the five per cent of pupils whose activities threaten to bring the teaching process to a halt. Meanwhile, the ordinary citizens – the large body of boys and girls who enjoy school – are neglected. Never has so much been done for so few at the expense of so many.

I do not lay the blame for all this on the youngsters who can see no purpose in it all. Their problems invariably originate in the home. Sad to say, they get some encouragement from certain branches of what are euphemistically called the supportive services. Many schools find that social workers act as the advocates and defenders of those who reject what is on offer.

The way out of the dilemma is to change the law. If a boy's teachers, plus his parents, plus the education officer, plus anyone else involved in his welfare are all agreed that he should leave school, would it not be sensible to let him go? Who will say no to that, and on what grounds?

This rational approach would release massive resources of money, time and energy to meet the needs of those who attend school willingly and whose inclination is to behave properly and who work to pass their examinations. Is it not time, perhaps, when they should have a square deal?

Ordinary children do not enjoy having wreckers among them. They would support what I am saying. So would ordinary parents. I don't mean the intelligentsia who send their children to my school for philosophical reasons, who are able to articulate their views and who have strong opinions about how the school should be run, sometimes welcome, sometimes not.

I am talking about the Mrs Dobsons of this world. Mrs D is my favourite parent, for all that one of her boys is not always a model of good behaviour. Her educational philosophy is ruggedly realistic, hewn from the rock of an ordinary parent's experience of life. She has sent all her sons to us and has told me: 'I'll tell you what I want you to do with 'em. I want you to learn 'em to read proper, write proper, add up proper and behave theirselves.' Inelegant that may be, but it sums up what most parents want from the schools to which the law requires them to send their offspring, namely the promotion of literacy, numeracy and civilized behaviour.

So, if we want to raise standards, here is how to do it. Change the law to allow freedom to those who demand it and invest what they have been absorbing in the needs of ordinary boys and girls. It is time we gave *them* justice.

TWO
THE MYTH THAT PARENTS
REALLY HAVE A CHOICE

It was said of Richard Nixon by one of his aides that watching him make decisions was like watching someone making sausages. When you saw what went into them, you lost your appetite.

Some of us have come to feel that way about how children are allocated to secondary schools, have we not? Seeing how it is done can be a nauseous experience. There are many worried parents faced with three alternatives.

One, to send their children to schools they don't want them to attend. Two, to buy private education. Three, to break the law and keep their children out of school until the authorities have a change of heart. All three have applied in my experience. Any system that presents people with that set of choices cannot be right and just.

Of course, the administrators are faced with an impossible task. How *do* you spread children between good and bad schools while attempting at the same time to give parents a free choice? It can't be done.

Every year, the largest of them – the Inner London Education Authority – claims that between 80 and 90 per cent of parents get their first choice of secondary school. What rubbish!

The system only works because the majority of people do what they are told and do not insist on having what they really want. If they were allowed unhindered freedom of selection between secondary schools, there would be chaos.

A great deal of antagonism arises from the fact that, when the authorities talk about parental choice, they don't mean what people think they mean.

Laurie Lee tells the story of his first day at school, which is relevant. Rescued from a playground fracas by a gracious lady teacher, he was told to sit in a certain place for the present. Having remained quietly and obediently all day in his allotted seat, he went home furious. 'What's the matter, Lol?' asked his sisters. 'She told me to sit there for the present but never gave it to me!' he complained.

When Winston Churchill was a young subaltern in South Africa, the water was not fit to drink. 'To make it more palatable', he later wrote, 'we had to add whisky. By diligent effort, I learned to like it.'

We have learned to like, or at least to live with, the various ways authorities have devised for transferring children from primary to secondary schools. We have done so for two reasons.

First, no political party wants to be the one to say the right of parental choice should be removed. Secondly, as long as the parents of bright children get more or less what they want, the boat will not be rocked too fiercely. But if you think about it, the children with the greatest learning difficulties need to be placed more carefully than those for whom learning is a doddle.

Even more to the point, the present system gives no special attention to that vast body of average children who constitute the largest section of the school population.

It is not, as some would say, the brightest pupils who are neglected, nor is it always the backward ones. The youngsters who, day by day, do themselves least justice in our education system – and have least justice done to them – are the ones in between.

When the writer Maurice Wiggin was a boy in a country school, the clever children were all right in the winter because they were allowed to sit at the back, where the hot water pipes were. The slow learners were also looked after: they sat at the front, near the boiler. Those who suffered, says Wiggin, were the poor little perishers in the middle.

How important is it to place the *average* young person in the right secondary school? What needs to be done to get their placement in some kind of proper order? The answer is that we should adopt the neighbourhood school. There are three principal reasons.

First, it would constitute an honest admission that genuine freedom of choice for all parents is impossible. Secondly, it would compel education authorities to face up to the aspirations of parents and act to *raise standards of teaching*. Thirdly, it would recognise that successful schools become neighbourhood schools anyway. The catchment area round a good school tightens all the time as it becomes more popular

Harry S Truman used to say, when he was President of the USA, that the art of leadership was persuading people to do what they should have done in the first place. The myth of parental choice is going to become more and more impossible as parents tumble to the truth. It is time to do what should have been done long ago. The future lies with the neighbourhood school.

THREE
ABOUT HEAD TEACHERS

Napoleon had a fine appreciation of leadership. When someone was recommended to him to be made an officer, he would ask: 'Is he lucky?' One thing is certain about being appointed a head teacher: you will have a hard time of it if fortune is not on your side. As often as not, those splendid moments when your unique visionary qualities are demonstrated for all to see arise simply from a happy coincidence of events over which you have no control.

And yet headship *does* involve the exercise of considerable power and immense influence. That being so, we ought to be more careful about how we appoint people to it. The least satisfactory feature of the present situation is the part played by local politicians. Some of them do not allow honest thought to penetrate the deep recesses in which their most cherished prejudices are preserved. Yet they expect to have an influence well beyond their competence.

In no other profession are the most senior appointments made by amateurs who possess that most devastating of all combinations – no understanding of what they are doing and total confidence in their ability to do it.

Speaking earlier this year at the annual conference of the Secondary Heads Association, an officer of the Inner London Education Authority found an apt phrase to describe the plethora of research documents reaching secondary heads: 'They sometimes remind me of stereophonic porridge – cold and grey and coming at you from all directions.' If we are to have food to meet our need, we will have to look beyond the question of how head teachers are appointed.

Equally important is the matter of how to bring headship to a conclusion. I'm not just talking about how to get rid of failures. A much bigger problem is that of providing opportunities for those who wish to move out after running schools successfully. This has become a critical issue with the appointment of very young men to top positions. Is it really in the best interests of the education system that they should remain *in situ* for a quarter of a century or more? The problem is not peculiar to the education system, but it has special implications there because children's lives will be affected by the way we handle it, or fail to do so.

'You're getting trouble from the headmaster? Organize a schoolkids picket of the gates. Even occupy his office. Come out of the darkness and join the fight.' This advice from the Socialist Workers Party to the young ladies and gentlemen of my establishment, issued in the street outside the school at the end of term, was thought outrageous by some of my colleagues and led a local resident to protest to the Department of Education and Science.

However, it is thoroughly consistent with general interest in the absorbing question of how to get rid of a head teacher – an interest quite often found among the teaching staff of a school.

Perhaps our cousins across the Atlantic have the right idea: don't appoint any. With disarming frankness, an American visitor told me: 'In the States, you know, we don't have guys like you.' Headship being the single most powerful position in our education system, it is not surprising that the occasional envious and/or critical glance is passed in its direction. Now the Government is to spend £100,000 on a three-year inquiry by Professor Ronald Glatter of the Open University into the way in which secondary heads are appointed.

The American political writer Theodore White tells of how ambitious politicians used to watch John F Kennedy when he was addressing a meeting in the hope of spotting his secret. They would lick their lips anxiously and lean forward in their seats, attempting to discern what special trick the great man was playing which they had somehow failed to acquire.

There are teachers who believe there is some special trick that is the key to achieving headship. Some are bitter because they feel cheated by a system that has failed to recognize their worth. Are they not as good as the next man? If only ...

You *do* have to be in the right place at the right time, and to come up against the right people. All of that depends to some extent on luck, as does being at your best at the critical hour. But those conditions apply to every one of life's great moments of judgment, from taking examinations to proposing marriage.

One thing of which every aspirant to headship needs to be aware is that, though acquiring one may be difficult, deciding that you have had enough of the slings and arrows of outrageous fortune that come with the job may be problematical. Some words of John Arden are appropriate:

> Who can tell how the lobster got
> Into the lobster pot?
> When he went in he did not doubt
> There was a passage out.
> But there was not.

Somebody's Child

Who is that child?
Scuffing the road with shoes too small, eyes
  too hard, not in school.
Miles away in his mind, seems cocksure, too
  cocksure.
Key of his place, chips in a bag, with nobody
  there.

Who is that child?
Riding the road with cast-off shoes, eyes too
  glazed, shuttered and marked.
Does what he's told, seems to hold on, he's
  holding on.
Never a space, just somewhere new, with
  nobody there.

Who is that child?
Trudging the road with combat boots, eyes
  too old, never young.
Hasn't learned to read and write, seems so
  angry, always angry.
A cardboard home, hand on the trigger, with
  nobody there.

Who is that child?
Trailing a road with crusty feet, eyes too big,
   belly too curved,
Bearing the woes of the next generation,
   seems so quiet, patiently yielding.
Heading for home, how many miles, with
   nobody there.

Are they yours?
Are they mine?

Where do we start, with nobody there?

Paula Elizabeth Dawson